# *THE*
## *JEWISH AMERICAN*

# PRINCE

## HANDBOOK

## Sandy Toback
## Debbie Haback

Illustrations by
L.T.W. Doney

First published October 1986

10   9   8   7   6   5   4   3   2   1

Manufactured in the United States of America

ISBN: 0-943084-47-4

Selected photos by Art Wise Studios

Excerpts from *Heartburn* by Nora Ephron
reprinted with permission of Alfred A. Knopf, Inc.
Copyright © 1983 by Nora Ephron.

Published by Turnbull & Willoughby Publishers, Inc.
1151 W. Webster
Chicago, IL 60614

To
Peter and Alan
with love.

## ACKNOWLEDGEMENTS

Randall Birnberg
Ronald Birnberg
David Duff
Robert Sherwin
Steve Kahn
Daniel Rose
Michael Barron
Linda Berman
Monica Klein
Eddy Smolin
Kurt Muller
Paul Pavur
Jeffrey Spitzer
Harry Tinowitz
Christine Stroebel
Patti Henebry
Gregg Robins
Gary Robins
Mindy Gansberg
Lou Robins
Susan Wolfe
Murry Barnett
Ricky Barnett
Rick Korn
Randy Kahan
Bernice Barnett
Mark Gurvitz
Marcy Kahan
Sheryl Lukatsky
Neeny Lukatsky
Sonny Kulatsky

Traci Haback
Amy Liss
Carrie Liss
Carol Goldstein
David Levy
Douglas Tumen
Shelly Kendall

# Table of Contents

# RACHEL SAMSTAT'S
# JEWISH PRINCE ROUTINE

**Exerpted from the
novel Heartburn by
Nora Ephron.**

You know what a Jewish prince is, don't you?
   *(Cocks her eyebrow)*
If you don't, there's an easy way to recognize one. A
simple sentence. "Where's the butter?"
   *(A long pause here, because the
   laugh starts slowly and builds)*
Okay. We all know where the butter is, don't we?
   *(A little smile)*
The butter is in the refrigerator.
   *(Beat)*
The butter is in the refrigerator in the little compartment
in the door marked "Butter."
   *(Beat)*
But the Jewish prince doesn't mean "Where's the but-
ter?" He means "Get me the butter." He's too clever to
say "Get me" so he ways "Where's."
   *(Beat)*
And if you say to him—
   *(Shouting)*
"in the refrigerator"—
   *(Resume normal voice)*
and he goes to look, an interesting thing happens, a
medical phenomenon that has not been sufficiently re-
marked upon.
   *(Beat)*
The effect of the refrigerator light on the male cornea.
   *(Beat)*
Blindness.
   *(A long beat)*
"I don't see it anywhere."
   *(Pause)*

"Where's the butter" is only one of the ways the Jewish
prince reveals himself. Sometimes he puts it a different
way. He says, "Is there any butter?"
   *(Beat)*
We all know whose fault it is if there isn't, don't we.
   *(Beat)*
When he's being really ingenious, he puts it in a way
that's meant to sound as if what he needs most of all
from you is your incredible wisdom and judgment and
creativity. He says, "How do you think butter would taste with this?"
   *(Beat)*
He's usually referring to dry toast.
   *(Beat)*
I've always believed that the concept of the Jewish prin-
cess was invented by a Jewish prince who couldn't get his
wife to fetch him the butter.

# Chapter One

# A
# PRINCE
# IS
# BORN

## The Prince in Training

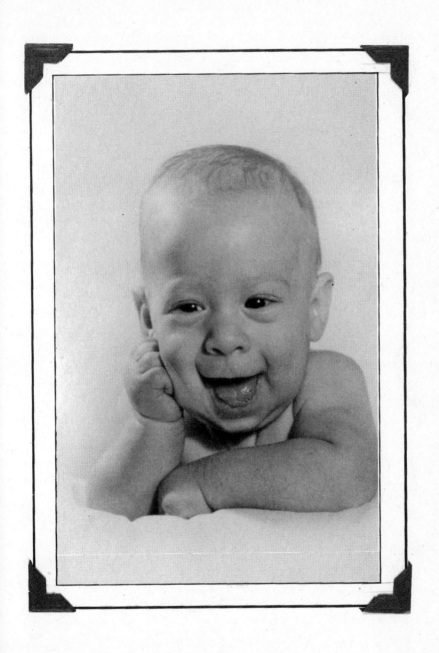

Rose and Myron Steinberg
announce the birth
of their son
David Michael
February 2, 1951
7 lbs. 10 oz.

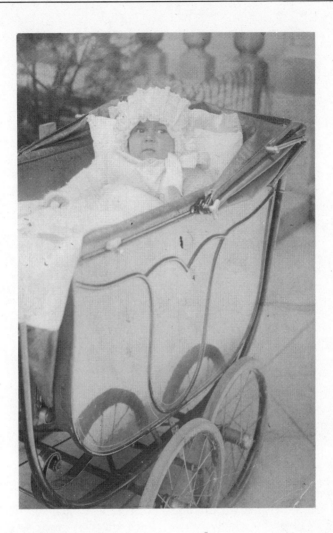

# The BRIS

An important initiation into the tribe is trial by circumcision. The *mohel* has been booked for months (just in case) and the caterer is on red alert (what, a new mother should cook?).

The 8th day after his birth is a joyous celebration for everyone but the tiny Prince.

Research into the annals of Hebrew history has revealed the true purpose of this ceremony. That momentary stab of pain is not only a covenent with God! It is a precursor to all the times, from that day on, when the women in the Prince's life — mother, wife, daughter — will also have him by the *baintzim*.

# A Prince By Any Other Name

Choosing the royal title shouldn't be taken lightly. The custom is to name the baby after a dear departed relative. Preferrably a successful one.

If Uncle Rubin was a top-notch banker, name your billion dollar baby Robbie. Robert is also a suitably distinguished name for a C.P.A. And Bob is right for the golf course. If you're raising a budding Supreme Court Justice, name him Michael after Grandpa Meyer, the Lebovitcher lawyer. These days, it's even more fitting to name a little Prince Zachary after his Great Aunt Zelda who was the first woman in her circle to wear pants in public. We know Zach will always wear the pants in his family.

In the 40's, Mort and Manny were derived from Moishe, the 60's saw Schecter turn to Scott. In the 70's, Josh was an appropriate appelation for Jacob's daughter's son. This tradition has come full circle. Young Princes currently enrolled in nursery school sound like old men at the schvitz . . . Moses, Aaron, Sam and Jake schmoozing over the sandbox.

Past and present baby boom parents
choose names like . . .

**Michael**

**David**

**Jeffery**

**Alan**

**Scott**

**Barry**

**Stuart**

**Jonathan**

**Joshua**

**Jay**

**Daniel**

**Steven**

Names never chosen:

**Skip**

**Chip**

**Kip**

**Tripp**

**Biff**

**Fritz**

**Lance**

**Terry**

**Patrick**

*The Little Macher*

# FATHER KNOWS BEST
## (Or So He Thinks)

No sooner has the young Prince entered the world, than the proud papa runs out to buy him a baseball, bat, mitt, football, helmet, *ad nauseum*. Meanwhile, mama is busy ordering *Black's Law Dictionary* and the *Physician's Desk Reference*. About the only thing they do agree on is early admission to Harvard, even though Boston is so gentile.

Thus begins the age-old battle for control of the Prince's destiny.

**Papa:**  Rose, look at that arm. He'll be another Sandy Koufax no less.

**Mama:**  Myron, those are the hands of a surgeon. No son of mine is going to make a living getting overheated from running around in circles.

**Papa:**  He's already overheated. You take him out in two sweaters, a hat and a snowsuit when it's 70 outside.

**Mama:**  Why are you talking such nonsense? He should be in a nice warm medical office. Or maybe the law library.

**Papa:**  It's not drafty in the law library?

**Mama:**  Sshhh Myron, did you hear that cry? Is he hungry? In pain? Maybe he caught a cold, *God forbid!* Shall I call Dr. Weiss?

**Papa:**  Leave David alone Rose. You're going to make him a mama's boy yet.

**Mama:**  *Now* you get the picture Myron.

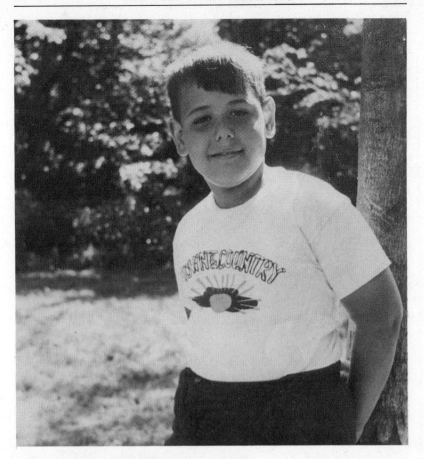

# SUMMERTIME:
# The Kosher Camps

The young Prince faces summer camp with mixed emotions. He can't wait to be on his own for eight weeks of hiking, swimming, sailing, horseback riding . . . all without fear of tracking dirt into the house. On the other hand, the prospect of eight weeks without mom catering to his every need might be a bit traumatic. But when the Prince thinks of all the girl campers on the other side of the lake, the scales tip in favor of summer camp.

In preparation, the young Prince stockpiles candy bars, comic book and even a Trojan stolen from his older brother. Mom packs insect repellent, aspirin, dramamine, calamine lotion and rubber rain boots. *These* items will probably come in handier considering that our young Prince is still wet behind the ears.

# LETTER FROM CAMP

Dear Mom and Dad.

Sorry I haven't written yet. Mom. I got your care package. Thanks for the rain boots. But we usually like to go barefoot when it rains. It's so fun to track mud in the cabin. My cold is almost gone.

Mom. don't read this part. Dad. did you ever hear of a panty raid? Last night a bunch of us guys snuck over to the girls side. The only problem was. our counselor got there before us. Was he ever mad when we caught him with Rachel. For punishment. he cancelled the preteen Shalom singles dance next Friday night.

Mom. read this. The best part of camp so far is color wars. They made me captain of the Blue team. Our team won every event but tennis. Guess all those years of lessons at the club were a waste.

You know what else? The food is great. We have P.B. & J.'s every day. They don't serve Spam like they do at Johnny Dolan's camp.

One thing really made me feel like home. We were at camp director Segal's cabin for a sing-along and his wife had plastic covers on all the furniture. I miss you. Mom.

Well. gotta go. Have to get ready for Shabbas services.

Love. Mark

P.S. When you come for Parents Day. please don't call me Markie and tell Grandma not to call me Bubbelah.

# PUPPY LOVE
## The Original Sin

The Prince learns early on that women are a pain in the you-know-what. They're always asking for something and never willing to give much back in return. But even so, from a tender age, the Prince can't help developing crushes on members of the opposite sex.

This makes the young Prince feel guilty. After all, shouldn't he love his mother best? She sacrificed everything for him and should always come first. Isn't that what she taught him?

But the lure is too great and the Prince just can't help himself. This leads to nurturing crushes in secret. His crushes turn to thoughts and feelings he just doesn't understand. About *this,* Mother never taught him! But as long as the object of his first affections are paper bunnies instead of females in flesh — can Mother really argue?

## Hiding Places For Playboy

In the attic

Under the bed

In the false ceiling in the utility room

In the garage behind the lawn furniture

At Sean O'Malley's house

In his older brother's room

In Dad's bathroom

In the Maid's closet

In the basement behind the furnace

In the smoked glass credenza in Mom's living room (no one ever goes there)

# The Sarah Complex:
# The Original Jewish Mother

Since time immemorial, Jewish mothers have been concerned with the best interests of their precious sons. Sarah, the first Jewish mother remembered by man, lived in a fashionable suburb in the Holy Land with her husband Abe.

Sarah and Abe were a happy couple who were having a little trouble conceiving. After 99 years, they decided to consult a specialist. He suggested they consider adoption. But this was impossible since they were the only Jewish people at the time and there were no Jewish babies available.

Finally they decided on a surrogate mother. Since artifical insemination was not an option for them, Abe chose Hagar as the surrogate and knew her in the biblical sense. The result was a bouncing baby boy named Ishmael.

Meanwhile, Sarah was finally able to relax and lo and behold, — she too, bore a son. They named him Isaac.

Sarah began to worry that Ishmael might be competition for her dar-

ling son, Isaac. Abe couldn't take her *draying* him about it all the time so he sent Hagar and Ishmael to live in the suburbs.

Life was pleasant for Sarah, Abe and Isaac. Soon, like all good fathers, Abe took Isaac to the annual Me and My Dad weekend outing. They left Sarah behind to play mah jong with the girls.

Abe and Isaac were enjoying a peaceful hike during the weekend when Abe's mobile cellular phone began to ring. It was the big boss calling. He demanded proof of Abe's loyalty by a sacrifice of his son, Isaac. Just before Abe was about to enroll Isaac in a future class at DeVry Institute of Technology, his phone rang again. The boss said that Abe had proven his loyalty. The boy could go to Wharton.

Abe, of course, told Sarah none of this. Another discussion about Isaac's future was more than he could handle.

# Chapter Two

# THE
# BAR MITZVAH

## And Other
## Adolescent Rituals

# HEBREW SCHOOL

From a parent's perspective, there's no better place to spend extracurricular time than in Temple. As for the Prince, he can think of any number of activities that would be more desirable, not the least of which would be cleaning his room. Hence, the Hebrew School Battle begins, each side claiming its own share of minor victories along the way, culminating in the Bar Mitzvah which is a major victory for everyone. Until that time, however . . . see if you can keep score . . .

## THE BIBLICAL BRIBE

Because a Hebrew education is so important, moms are willing to make major sacrifices to keep their boychicks behind school doors. They're even willing to go to such lengths as permitting their Princes to play football a few nights a week (God forbid he should break a bone!), in exchange for the Prince's promise that he will learn his *aleph bets.*

## THE BAIT AND SWITCH

Princely parents often try appealing to the Prince's sense of guilt. "How will you pass the tradition on to your children if you know nothing about you're Jewish Heritage?" they *drey.* So it's off to

Hebrew School for the young Prince. But when he comes home asking why his mom is making cheeseburgers? She replies, "OK Mr. smarty pants . . . forget the cheeseburgers, *and* forget the ice cream I brought home for dessert. I'll give you *Milchich* and *Fleishich!"*

## THE TRADE OFF

There are, believe it or not, worse fates in life than Hebrew School. Running three miles with the team after football practice is worse torture than spending three hours slumped over a Hebrew primer in class. When the Prince's mom picks him up and sees all the guys looking at him with envy, he tells her that it's because they're just jealous of the fine education she's providing him with, not that they're jealous he's getting out of running. If she catches on, she may double his torture and return him to the track to continue running around in circles.

## THE SHILL

If the Prince must go to Hebrew School, it shouldn't be a total loss. The decrepit old *bubbes* who teach are easy marks for the prankster Prince. He can perfect his spitball, rubber band shooting and note

passing techniques, behind these biblical biddies backs. Soon the Prince will master these "skills" well enough to try them out in junior high the next day on teachers made of sterner stock.

## THE STRONG ARM

There's always one Prince who actually appears to *enjoy* Hebrew School. (He's actually just obsessed with being the best at everything and, of course, all of his friends hate his guts.) He's even the one who volunteers to go to extracurricular Saturday services. But he often encounters an extracurricular fight on the way home. You've got to be as tough as a piece of *gedempte fleish* to be good in Hebrew School.

## CONFESSIONS FROM THE CHEDER

I was always too afraid to ditch Hebrew School. And now I know why. My friends were trying to convince me I'd never get caught . . . and I finally believed them. So, one afternoon, the guys and I snuck off to the mall. We had a great time goofing around. I threw all caution to the wind and even bought an album. I could always say I borrowed it. I got home right on time that night. So far, so good. As usual, Mom was waiting for me in the kitchen. But her customary smile was replaced by a frightening scowl. "How was Hebrew School?" she asked. "Fine, I replied." "I hate when you lie," she admonished. And I freaked out. How could she know? It was my first time. If she had been born 300 years ago, she'd have been burned at the stake. But no, it's my life at stake, and she's not a witch, she's just a bitch. And doesn't it figure that I'd leave my wallet at Rainbow Records. Sometimes honesty just doesn't pay. But when it comes to my mother I always do. If the clerk had been a crook, I'd be off the hook.

**Randy Nusbaum**
**Shaker Heights**

# THE ROYAL SUMMONS

My parents and I would be honoured to have you worship with us on the occasion of my Bar Mitzvah on Saturday, the sixteenth of May, Nineteen hundred and seventy, at nine o'clock in the morning. Ner Tamid Congregation, Twenty-seven fifty-four West Rosemont Avenue, Chicago, Illinois.

Please join us for dinner on Sunday the seventeenth of May, six o'clock in the evening, at the Hyatt House, Lincolnwood, Illinois.

Michael Jay Barron

Black Tie Optional

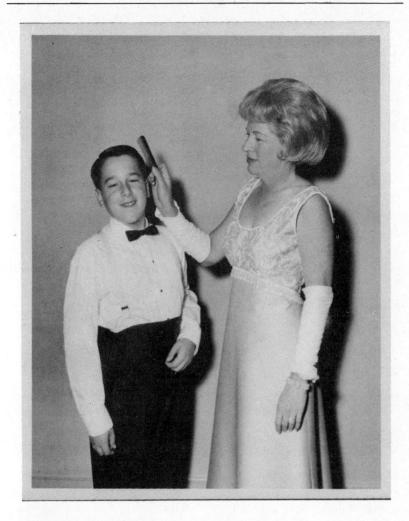

# MOTHER'S LITTLE JEWEL

At last the big day is here. Mother's little jewel is finally a Bar Mitzvah. With weapon in hand, mom applies the finishing touches. The symbols of manhood are much in evidence — from the look of bravado to the look of his tuxedo. Only moments from now the Princeling will step into that sacred arena. Now if only he can think about chanting his haftorah and not about dancing with Laura later that night.

Advice to Bar Mitzvah mom: Enjoy combing those lovely locks — they'll be lost forever by his wedding day.

# It's My Party

If the Bar Mitzvah boy shines during the temple service, his mother shines at the parties that follow. She's been planning for this day for over two years, ever since the date was assigned. And, oh what a day it is!

**8:00 am** Wake up, excited about Saturday morning little league game.

**8:30 am** Appear for breakfast in team uniform.

**8:35 am** Realize everyone else is dressed for a party.

**8:36 am** Realize it's your party.

**8:37 am** Mother reaches for the Valium. "What are you dressed in? Where do you think you're going?"

**8:38 am** Run upstairs to change into your new Polo Bar Mitzvah suit.

**8:45 am** Leave for temple.

**8:50 am** Turn back — forgot speech at home.

**9:15 am** Arrive at temple

**9:30 am** Service begins.

**11:30 am** Service ends, mother pops another valium.

**11:45 am** Checks start coming in.

**11:50 am** Bar Mitzvah consultant stops you and your friends from pushing each other into the ladies room.

**11:51 am** Just in time as mother comes looking for you to drag you off to talk to great aunt Frieda, (the one that gives $15 checks).

**12:00 pm** Luncheon is served. Lox and bagels, smoked sable, whitefish and sturgeon. Pickled herring. Gefilte fish. Honey Cake . . . all your favorites. Good thing there's a dinner party at the country club tonight.

**2:00 pm** Home at last. Count checks with Dad while watching a baseball game on TV.

**2:15 pm** Mom runs out for a comb out and a touch up from her manicurist, with a quick stop at the drug store for a refill on Valium.

**6:00 pm** Time to leave for the country club. Everyone tells you how handsome you look in your first tuxedo.

**6:15 pm** Mother has last minute anxiety over the hors d'oeuvres selection. You have last minute anxiety over who to select for the first dance.

**7:15 pm** You get your first taste of working the crowd as dozens of pre-teen girls and post menopausal matrons vie for your attention.

**7:30 pm** Silver salvers of roast beef come rolling into the dining room.

**8:00 pm** All too soon it's time for the first dance. Judi Silverman is the lucky lady. She's looking good, except, wait, a bit of Kleenex is peeking out from her attempt at cleavage. A last minute switch to Heidi Applebaum. *(Her's is the real thing.)*

**8:15 pm** Dancing on air. So what if Heidi is four inches taller and your mother is giving you a dirty look. The other guys are green with envy.

**10:30 pm** After a seemingly endless set of Hokey Pokey, the Bunny Hop and the *Hora,* the sweet table is set out.

**11:00 pm** Your friends start a food fight with the croque en bouche. Mother pops another Valium.

**12:00 pm** Dad carries mother out of the room. You relax on the brocade sofa. The photographer snaps a picture. The greatest day of your life is over. At least you have next Saturday's little league to look forward to.

# THE BAR MITZVAH ALBUM

**Man of the hour!**

**Two for the price of one!**

# THE BAR MITZVAH SPEECH

## THANK YOU ALL FOR COMING . . .

Rabbi, Cantor, parents, relatives, friends. I would like to welcome all of you who have come to share with me one of the most important days of my life (tomorrow will really be the most important day 'cause all of this will be over). I hope we'll all have many more simchas to celebrate together. (Like next week's little league play offs.)

I want to thank my parents, grandparents, sister, brother, aunts and uncles who have instilled in me those values that will enable me to enter adulthood with maturity and clear thinking. (Yeah, like greed, I hope cousin Shlomo doesn't give his usual $5.00 check like Mom complained he would!) I have learned to conduct my life in a manner that will make my family proud.

And now as I venture forth into adulthood with all its trials and tribulations (will Linda let me feel her up, after all it is MY Bar Mitzvah?), and I am confident that I will be able to make wise decisions (is she wearing a front or back hook bra?)

My education in Judaism has prepared me to face whatever challenges come my way (like finishing my thank you notes before the postage goes up.)

In conclusion, I would like to say thank you to all of you for helping me to mark this important milestone. (Yeah! No more Hebrew School.) AMEN!

# Chapter Three

# RISKY PRINCE-NESS

## The Teen Years

# Hell On Wheels

## (To the Tune of "Born to be Wild")

Head out on the Parkway
Looking for a *shiksa*
And whoever comes my way
Born to be *vilde*

State of
**New York**
Driver's License

1986

1987

Bruce J. Tannenbaum
123 Royal Lane
Princeton, New Jersey

Eyes:       brown
Hair:       curly
Height:     tall enough so dates can wear heels
Sex:        plenty before marriage
Birthdate:  the happiest day in his mother's life

His 16th birthday marks the Prince's true liberation. The key to this liberation fits his very own Camero, Firebird, Trans Am, Mustang, Cutlass or GTO — the long awaited surprise birthday gift.

Of course, receiving a car is really no surprise to the Prince. He's been planning for these hot wheels of his own ever since he was old enough to play doctor in the back seat of Marsha Greenberg's father's Buick.

# VEHICULAR VERNACULAR

A Crash Course for the Prince

**Cruising:** Looking for chicks but never stopping long enough to be caught by one.

**Laying a Patch:** Making a permanent mark on the pavement — not on his girlfriend.

**Burning Rubber:** A use for this substance after a night of heavy petting goes up in smoke.

**4-Wheel Drive:** The process of the Prince and three friends deciding where to take the evening's joy ride.

**Shotgun:** The thought of Rachel's dad holding one of these to a Prince's head prevents things from getting too steamy in his new sportscar.

**Hang a Reggie:** The proper action when spotting a Woody Wagon full of blonde, blue-eyed St. Mary's coeds turning right on Main Street.

**Hang a Louie:** The proper action when spotting Lila Feldstein and her friends turning right on Main Street.

**Chinese Fire Drill:** A way to let all the cute JAP girls know that you really do have legs and that you do get out of your car every now and again.

## Cooped Up in a Coupe DeVille

I thought my worst nightmare was about to come true when I heard mom and dad discussing handing mom's crummy Cadillac over to me instead of trading it in for the sporty new convertible (that I consider to be my birthright). I imagined the guys jeering as I would drive by in that awful old Jew Canoe. And besides, I'm too young to be behind the wheel of that big boat, I still have all my own hair.

Thank God my Uncle Morrie — who has a car dealership in Yonkers — made them a really great deal on a new Cutlass. Of course, I had to promise Uncle Morrie that I'd take his wife's cousin Alissa as my first date on wheels . . . but what's a Prince to do?

**Jay Birnbaum**
**Tarrytown**

# THERE'S A FIRST TIME FOR EVERYTHING

 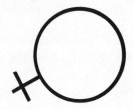

In the 3rd grade, I noticed girls, but I hated them. In the 6th grade, I was afraid of them. By the 7th grade, I was interested in them, but I only wanted to look, not touch. How Gross!

At 14, I had my first big night on the town with Tony Vissotto and his dad. We went to the Wild Kitten Strip Joint, where the mysteries of the female anatomy were revealed to me by Puss E. Kat. What she could do with tassles! The rumors I'd heard in the locker room were finally confirmed. Now I wanted to look *and* touch . . .

At last, at age 16, I got my chance while attending my cousins's Bar Mitzvah party in Manhattan. Bored, I wandered into the hotel bar, sat down and ordered a screwdriver, the only drink I had ever heard of. I hadn't been there 15 minutes when an older woman, she must — have been at least 22 — sat down right next to me. "I saw you leaving" she said, "that Bar Mitzvah's really a drag. So many little kids." She asked if I was in from school. I lied and said I was in my first year of med school. What a coincidence, she was a nurse. Uhch, now I'm in big trouble. But I got a reprieve, she said she didn't want to talk about work on the weekend. My reprieve was short-lived, however. She asked me up to her room. I figured, what the hell, there's a first time for everything.

Up in her room, she asked if I wanted another drink. I knew I needed it to fortify myself for what was sure to come next. While we were waiting for room service, she started taking off my shirt. I realized this was going to be the big moment. When that realization came, so did I. She didn't seem to mind my eagerness and the rest of the afternoon is one I'll always remember! And so will all my friends who I think are starting to get sick of hearing this story.

**Jordy Gumble**
**Bexley, Ohio**

# TEEN TOUR
# If it's Tuesday, this must be Tel Aviv.

As reward for making the grade in high school — as if there were any question — the Prince's parents send him packing off to Europe and the Holy Land! But would any Jewish mother be able to stand thinking of her son roaming in Rome without the proper supervision? Hence, the guided teen tour.

Twenty-five young royals, led by a Hebrew school teacher type, embark on a journey through the capitals of Europe ending up in Jerusalem beside the wailing wall. Their mothers would be the ones wailing if they knew what really happens on these high school holidays!

While pretending to concentrate on the portraits in the National Gallery, the sculptures in the Prado and the paintings in the Louvre, the Prince is thinking of other things.

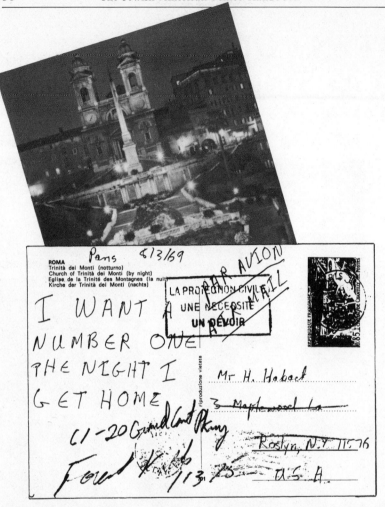

# Places to sneak off to on the teen tour.

**Paris**
Place Pigalle — less embarassing for Prince. No need to talk to non-english speaking hookers.

**London**
To Chuck and Di's for tea. A Princely tete a tete.

**Amsterdam**
Red light district is a real turn on. Also turn on with space cakes from Das Milky Vay.

**Florence**
Ponte Vecchio post midnight. Former flower children help the Prince relive the psychodelic 60's.

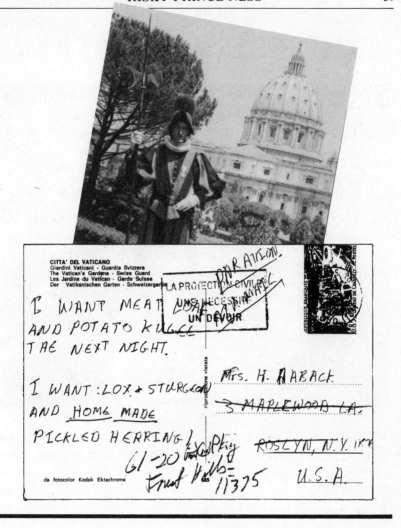

CITTA' DEL VATICANO
Giardini Vaticani - Guardia Svizzera
The Vatican's Gardens - Swiss Guard
Les Jardins du Vatican - Garde Suisse
Der Vatikanischen Garten - Schweizergarde

I WANT MEAT LOAF
AND POTATO KUGLL
THE NEXT NIGHT.

I WANT: LOX + STURGEON
AND *HOME MADE*
PICKLED HERRING

Mrs. H. AABACK
3 MAPLEWOOD LA.
ROSLYN, N.Y. 11375
U.S.A.

da fotocolor Kodak Ektachrome

## Rome
Trevi Fountain — Practice pinching the roman beauties.

## Monte Carlo
In his Bar Mitzvah tux, the Prince might be able to cajole his way into a casino.

## Stockholm
Anywhere in town. Capital of *free* love. The Prince's heritage makes him a sucker for *anything* when the price is right?

## Vienna
The Hotel New Hampshire

## Mykonnos
Sneak a peak at a topless beach.

## Brussels
Even at an early age, the prince can't resist a deal on diamonds.

# THE PROM PROBLEM

Warning to Jewish Princes: Don't ever think you can outfox your mother. Here's a cautionary tale to prove this point.

It was the best of times, it was the worst of times. It was prom time. And also time to look for a date. I looked no further than the seat in front of me, where sat the luscious Colleen Kelley. We'd been friends all year, but I was always afraid to ask her out. What would· my mother say. The prom was my last chance. In a crazy moment of passion, I popped the question. She accepted instantly. And, in that instant, my troubles began. What was I going to tell my mother? Not the truth!

I concocted an elaborate scheme about my plans for the prom weekend. To throw my mother off the track, I told her I started going steady with Marlene Glassman, so when prom time came my choice for a date would be obvious. Most mothers could care less about their son's high school flings. Only *my* mother wanted to meet mine. I kept putting her off until it just became easier to let Marlene in on my scheme and ask for her co-operation. Marlene even came for dinner!

At last prom weekend arrived. De-- spite my mother's pleas that Marlene and I come back to the house for pictures, I said time was tight and promised to take pictures of us at the dance. Unfortunately, pictures *were* taken at the dance, and I was captured with Colleen on Kodachrome.

When my mom asked to see the prom pictures, I instantly concocted another story, saying that Marlene and I broke up, and Marlene was so mad at me that she ripped up all the pictures and burned the negatives.

But leave it to my wiley mother. One afternoon, at her weekly Mah Jong game, Joyce Edelman showed the "girls" her son's prom pictures. Of course my eagle-eyed mother immediately spotted Colleen and I, and came straight home to confront me. She caught me just like the proverbial animal in a trap. I had to admit my guilt. Thank God I was going to college 2,000 miles away.

Moral of the story: Hell hath no fury like a mother scorned, especially for a *shiksa*.

# Chapter Four

# THE STUDENT PRINCE

## Higher Education — It's a Matter of Degree

# SCOUTING FOR SCHOOLS
## The Undergrad Dilemma

Perhaps the biggest decision thus far in the young Prince's life is which college will be right for him. You'd think his mother was going with him, the way she agonizes over the whole thing. She, of course, wants her Prince to be within driving distance so she can still do his laundry and make him dinner once a week. He, The Prince, just wants to be distant, so long as he's not too distant from a girls dorm.

The Prince must choose a college that will properly prepare him for stepping into his father's shoes (and his office), for passing his CPA exam (in case going on to law school is a passing fancy), to ensure a bankable future (as a banker, he'll be investing in a secure future).

Naturally, the Prince lives on campus. His idea of a commuter school means a cross country train ride, lest his mother show up for a surprise visit. But, proximity to girls, though important, is usually a secondary concern for the academic Prince. With that in mind, — here are his choices.

## American University
Washington D.C. (5,149 students)

For the ever-politic Prince. Major to choose is Government Affairs. An affair with a page from the Hill could make life more interesting. Pack your tuxedo and subscribe to *Commentary*.

## Boston University
Boston, Massachusetts (15,000 students)

700 is the place to live, not how many Princesses you should try to date freshman year. Close enough to Ivy Leagues to make grad school interviews convenient. Pack Preppy. It doesn't hurt to look like the locals. You never know when Brahmin will invite you home for dinner.

## University of Chicago
Chicago, Illinois (6,080 students)

Be the coolest, best looking guy on campus. The school for nerd academicians. Plastic pocket protector di rigeur. Favorite Saturday night activity . . . recharging calculators.

## Tulane
New Orleans, Louisiana (3,104 students)

For Social Princes. Date your way through Newcomb. Go Greek. Be prepared for late nights out. Acquire a taste for Bourbon and Bourbon Street.

## U.C.L.A.
Los Angeles, California (20,796 students)

Academics are top-notch. All of California is your vacation playground. Blonde beach bunnies abound everywhere but on campus.

Pack your JAMS and learn how to surf for weekends in Malibu.

## University of Miami
Coral Gables, Florida (8,276 students)

Preferred major — Pre-father's business. Flashy sports car a must for forays into Coconut Grove. Pack your Miami Vice look — the maid won't be around to iron for you.

## University of Colorado
Denver, Colorado (12,000 students)

Break your mother's heart by going to the Rockies. Don't break your neck by skiing them. Pack extra sweaters! You'll need them! What do Princes know from cold? Main reasons for attending — to put distance between you and your parents.

## University of Illinois
Champaign/Urbana, Illinois (35,628 students)

Largest Greek population anywhere — outside of Athens. Sammies, ZBT's, TEP's, AEPi's and Tau Delts, in that order. Pack Brains. Princely competition is fierce.

## Arizona State
Tempe, Arizona (19,780 students)

Grades inversely proportionate to suntan. Acceptable starter car a must. Pack golf clubs for all day "study sessions".

## Brandeis
Boston, Massachusetts (6,250 students)

Better than Harvard. More NJG's per squre foot. Entire student body has nose jobs . . . and noses in the air.

## Columbia
New York, New York (8,000 students)

Settle into upper west side. Establish yuppiedum early. Women, Wall Street and good delis all within reach. Pack plastic. Big weekends cost big bucks.

Albany, New York (15,000 students, Podiating is favorite pastime. Intramural sports a must. V-Football a no-no. Future CPA's abound. Frats Forbidden. Sutter's for Sabbath. Pack your parka, it's been known to snow in May.

# Forbidden Fruit

**Notre Dame**
Football is such an un-Princely sport.

**Loyola (all of them)**
Nix any school founded by Jesuits.

**Valparaiso**
For the location alone.

**Southern Methodist University**
Need we say more.

**Baylor**
Just take our word for it.

**Holy Cross College**
Imagine one hanging around your neck.

**West Point**
What's the point. Princes do not join the armed forces.

# CHOOSING A MAJOR

When selecting a college curriculum, the Prince has a myriad of options from which to choose . . . as long as he chooses pre-law, pre-med or accounting.

Of course, the Prince has many people besides himself to think of when deciding on his courses. It goes without saying, but let's say it anyway, that first and foremost he must consider his mother. What will make her *kvell* with pride? His father's wishes must be weighed, or who will finance this endeavor? And last, but not least, he must make a choice that will not blow his chances of being chosen himself by a Nice Jewish Girl.

Once his decision is made, the Prince pursues his studies with a religious fervor. He and his fellow Princes always set the curve. And speaking of curves, the Prince always adds a few gut courses to his schedule. This will enable him to come into close contact with blonde *shiksa* sorority sisters who obviously won't be in any of his other classes.* By the time finals roll around, the Prince will have scored high marks with Mary Beth, as well as with his professors. Being at the top of his class prepares him for being at the top of his chosen profession.

## *CONFIDENTIAL NOTE TO PRINCESSES:

Dr. Johnathan Waxman, Johns Hopkins '79, was the one known exception to this rule. He actually met a sumptuous blonde Baptist who had not only beauty but brains as well. While dissecting frogs in bio 101 he also dissected her personality and eventually married her. Naturally she converted. But don't give up hope smart Princesses. As stated, this story is merely an exception to the rule.

Even with tempting blonde bombshells coming on to the Prince, (don't all mothers tell their daughters that Jewish men make the best husbands?) his education still comes first. No wonder the library is the best place to meet a Prince. Don't worry girls, even with his nose in a book, the Prince can still sense an alluring perfume. Princes are only human, even though their mothers tell them otherwise.

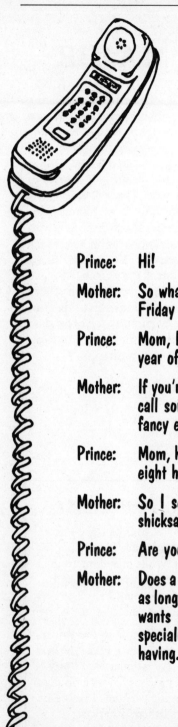

## DIAL A GUILT TRIP

**Prince:** Hi!

**Mother:** So what's the big shot doctor doing home on a Friday night?

**Prince:** Mom, I'm not a doctor yet. This is only my first year of med school. How's Dad?

**Mother:** If you're so worried about your father, you could call sometime. After all, he is paying for your fancy education.

**Prince:** Mom, how do you expect me to call when I spent eight hours last night working on my cadaver?

**Mother:** So I see that you're still dating that anorexic shicksa.

**Prince:** Are you calling for a reason?

**Mother:** Does a mother need a reason to call her son? But as long as I've got you on the phone, Aunt Phyllis wants me to ask you if she should consult a specialist about some chest pains she's been having.

**Prince:** Mom, you don't have to be a doctor to know that she's got heartburn. The schmaltz and onion sandwiches she eats for lunch could kill an ox.

**Mother:** Darling, we'll be seeing you for Seder won't we?

**Prince:** Only if you look at my Bar Mitzvah picture. I've got too much work and exams are the following week.

**Mother:** Well it's too bad you're not coming home because I've invited Marlene Lieberman's daughter and she's turned into such a beauty.

**Prince:** Mom, I told you, I don't have time. And besides, isn't she the one who used to go to Weight Watcher camp every summer?

**Mother:** I get such a headache listening to your *bubbemeisas*.

**Prince:** OK Mom, then hang up, take two aspirins and call don't call me in the morning.

# THE GREAT DEBATE:
# Law School vs. Med School vs. Business School

Since the days of Solomon, Princes have been pondering which path to take in life. To those of you who haven't decided yet (what the heck are you waiting for, your indecision is probably *killing* your mother!), this handy chart could help you make up your mind.

|  | Lawyer | Doctor | Businessman |
|---|---|---|---|
| Entry into real world delayed | 3 years | 6 years | 2-6 years |
| You are a: |  |  |  |
| Smooth Talker | Yes | No | Yes |
| Snappy Dresser | Yes | No | Yes |
| Shrewd Manipulator | Yes | No | Yes |
| You have: |  |  |  |
| Good Beside Manor | No | Yes | Yes |
| All Your Own Hair | No | No | No |
| A Good Golf Game | Yes | Yes | Yes |
| You want to: |  |  |  |
| Make A Fortune | Yes | Yes | Yes |

# CAREER TRAINING
## The Varsity Squad

Pity the poor Prince. He's too short to play basketball. Too scrawny to play football. Too in-debt to the orthodontist to play hockey. Besides, who ever heard of a designer football jersey? Nevertheless, the Prince *can* score big in varsity sports.

Tennis and golf are the names of the games. The Prince approaches these games in the same way he'll approach a business deal in later years — with objectives, strategies and tactics.

The bottom line:
Don't worry Princes, no one will think you're a wimp for not carrying the pigskin or dribbling down the court. How many great deals were negotiated while in a gridlock?

# THE PRINCELY PLEDGE

The collegiate Prince joins a fraternity for the same reasons his father joins a country club: Acceptance into an elite group, a built-in social life and a chance to play sports. What's more, the food is far better than the standard dorm fare (where SPAM is the dietary staple).

Pledging starts with the infamous "Rush Weekend" i.e. ZBT's Taco and Tequila, or AEPi's Midnight Madness. A dozen or so high school seniors are invited to the frathouse for a weekend of partying with the brothers during which they get their first taste of the cameraderie of fraternity life: Drinking until they throw up, dating DG's, sleeping with strangers (don't get excited, it's only other pledges), taking cold showers (for medical purposes) and smoking dope until their lungs beg for mercy. In fact, pledging a fraternity is the closest thing these NJB's ever get to joining the armed forces!

Being a Sammie, Zeeb or Ape pledge is no fun. In fact, it may be *worse* than joining the army. Not only do the pledges have to keep track of their own goings on, they have to keep tabs on the actives, too. Making their own beds and their big brother's too, attending class in lieu of big brother, washing big brother's car on the off-chance of borrowing it and cleaning up after *every* party. And it's not even Hell Week yet!

This may all sound like a drag — and it is — but the positives far outweigh the negatives. Girls! Girls! Girls!

Fraternity life is synonymous with social life. Every weekend brings a party and/or a dance. socially inept pledges appreciate hundreds of girls arriving at their doorstep every weekend. Too bad they're all looking for upperclassmen.

But soon the pledges' day will come. For that reason, they observe their big brother techniques very carefully. Bragging, showing off, treating dates like they don't exist, etc. Somehow these methods seem to work. Efforts at post-party pledge cleanup are often thwarted by groping couples littered about the house.

The only way left for the pledges to release their frustrations is through interfraternity sports — baseball, soccer, basketball and hockey. The Prince has a chance to excell competing with his fellow greeks as he never would in varsity sports. What's more, the shicksa sorority sisters drool over *boychicks* with biceps.

In later years, the Prince who doesn't dial his own phone, put his own ice in the glass, or God forbid, pick up his own socks or ever live within two acres of his closest neighbor looks back on his fraternity days as the high point of his existence.

# THE COLLEGIATE

Why would the Prince prefer this room to his nice clean interior decorator's dream room at home, where the maid always picked up after him? At school, he must take a date to dinner and a show before she'll ever even deign to move his books off the bed before she sits on it, much less straighten up the entire room for him. But even a princely pig sty is preferable to a room as neat as a pin with his mother always sticking her nose in.

1. Golf Clubs

2. Tennis racket

3. Softball

4. Expensive stereo component clock radio

5. Posters: Poverty Sucks, Choices, Dogs Playing Poker

6. Twin beds with navy and brown sheets and comforters

7. Do Not Disturb sign from the Concord (used to warn roommate that passion is in session)

# PRINCE'S ROOM

8. Cassettes stacked to the ceiling
9. Compact Disc player
10. Bong filled with stale Manischewitz (also other related paraphenalia)
11. Dirty sock collection
12. Stack of Playboy, Penthouse, Time and Forbes for john reading
13. Afghan knitted by high school girlfriend
14. Color TV with cable
15. Address book categorized by bust measurements
16. Aramis and Polo cologne and after shave

17. Anti nuke banner
18. Candles (for romantic interludes)
19. List of old girlfriends' phone numbers
20. List of potential girlfriends' phone numbers
21. Full bar
22. Millions of albums
23. Couches from second hand store
24. Ex-girlfriend's picture
25. Big Ten Girls calendar

# HOUSE HUNTING

| | SAMMIES |
|---|---|
| Sleeping accommodations | Freshman dorms — perfect for voyeurs and exhibitionists |
| Dope connections | A source of income for these junior entrepreneurs |
| Dating preference (what they want) | Thetas, DGs, Alpha Chis, Kappas |
| Dating habits (what they get) | AEPhis |
| Japmobiles | BMW, Mercedes 190E, Prelude |
| Income/Career goals | Rich |

# WAITING FOR LADIES

I, who had never so much as carried a dish to the sink while I was growing up, found myself waiting tables at AEΦ. How it happened, I'll never know. What I do know is that Mike Brodsky made an announcement at dinner about a great way of meeting girls. The very next night I found myself with 100 gossiping girls, all with their own personal bottle of diet salad dressing. What a

| ZBT | AEPi |
|---|---|
| Private rooms — these guys don't share anything | Double rooms — at least if you don't have a date you won't be alone on the weekend |
| Mushrooms are a dietary staple | The scales tip in their favor |
| Pi Phis, Tri Delts, Thetas, Kappas | Phi Mus, Thetas, an occasional GDI |
| Townies | SDTs |
| RX7, Trans Am, Mustang Convertible | 300ZX, Celica, Camero |
| Richer | Richest |

switch for someone who always had his mother and sisters at his beck and call. But my hard work paid off. Between the main course and dessert, I spotted a real dish: Tanya Rabinowitz was beautiful, with her own nose, yet. The moment we met was destiny. I was destined to spend my entire allowance on her. She was destined to fix up all her sorority sisters with my fraternity brothers. Unfortunately, Tanya was all show and no go. But I couldn't admit that to the guys in the house. So we continued to date, while I carried on my pretense. And, believe me, things haven't gotten any better since I gave her the ring. And that was five years ago!

**David Traptman**
**Brandeis '80**

# DISPLAYING THE DEGREE
## Techniques of Diplomacy

**The Snuggler:** His diploma is sure to keep him warm while dreaming of cold cash.

**The Stroller:** He knows he'll soon be struttin' down easy street with this sheepskin.

**The Seeker:** This graduate Prince is ready to forge right into the real world.

**The Mad Doctor:** Those big eyes are mad for the money he'll make.

When the Prince finally wrests his diploma away from his mother (who had had it in her clutches since graduation day) he feels compelled to display it to his friends and colleagues. Here is a quick look at the best techniques of diplomacy.

**The Cash and Carry:** This Prince can afford to look smug. Soon he'll be carting off big bucks.

**The Scowl:** For all of those who doubted he would ever make it.

Soon the Prince's diploma will be proudly displayed on his wall where it proves he's the success his mother always knew he would be.

# Chapter Five

# PRINCE OF THE CITY

## The Book of Job(s)

# CHARTING THE PRINCE'S CAREER COURSE

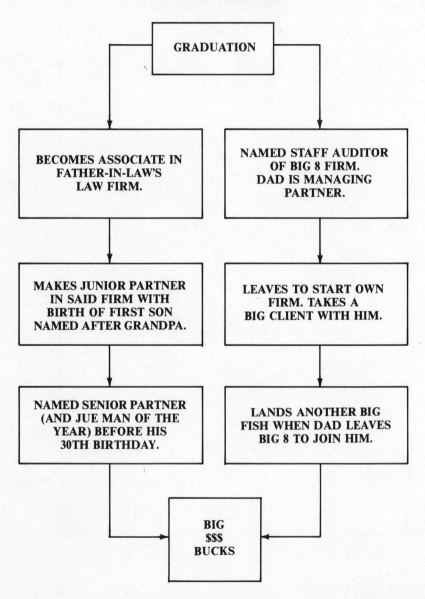

GRADUATION

BECOMES ASSOCIATE IN FATHER-IN-LAW'S LAW FIRM.

NAMED STAFF AUDITOR OF BIG 8 FIRM. DAD IS MANAGING PARTNER.

MAKES JUNIOR PARTNER IN SAID FIRM WITH BIRTH OF FIRST SON NAMED AFTER GRANDPA.

LEAVES TO START OWN FIRM. TAKES A BIG CLIENT WITH HIM.

NAMED SENIOR PARTNER (AND JUE MAN OF THE YEAR) BEFORE HIS 30TH BIRTHDAY.

LANDS ANOTHER BIG FISH WHEN DAD LEAVES BIG 8 TO JOIN HIM.

BIG $$$ BUCKS

# ENTRY LEVEL
## Starting at the Top

Every Princely college grad has a vision of himself, ten years down the road, ensconced in a luxurious office behind a door that bears his name. The Prince's mother has this vision as well. And has had it since the day her darling entered the world. Most men begin their careers in the mail room, as an assistant to the assistant or as some other lower level functionary. Not so the Prince.

The roadblocks that other mortal men must encounter to reach the zenith of their careers have already been removed by the Prince's proud parents during his formative years. Friends and relatives all vie to have the Prince come to work for them.

Just think how many new clients/customers/patients will be signed up from among the Prince's parents' crowd.

If the Prince becomes a lawyer, his parents' cronies will line up to have the Prince negotiate, sue or settle. Should the Prince become a doctor, relatives will keep him busy examining, prescribing and stitching. Even if the Prince becomes a hairdresser (God forbid), he'll have an enormous clientele waiting to be shampooed, set and snipped.

Do we detect a little nepotism here? Well yes, but justifiably so. The Prince's parents were always *dreying* him to be a hardworker in school all these years. After all of their pressure and praise, he is convinced that his innate intelligence and *savior faire* can get him through any situation. Hence, starting at the top is standard operating procedure for the Prince.

# TOP TEN
# PRINCELY PROFESSIONS

The Prince's persona is defined by his profession . . . everything he is, everything he says, everything he does, everything people think about him. It all hinges on the field he chooses for amassing his fortune.

But not just any ordinary job will do. The right career must be able to:

1. Guarantee a six figure income within five years.
2. Generate five hours of impressive party conversation.
3. And preferably provide the right initials after his name.

Here's a run down of acceptable careers where Princes can make the most of their diplomas. (The most money, that is.)

## C.P.A.

This practical Prince spends his entire life accounting for how other people spend their money. His career begins at one of the big eight. Upon making partner, the Prince leaves to start his own firm where his son will join him one day.

## DOCTOR

The Prince who dedicates himself to this career can heal the wounds inflicted on his long suffering mother when he was young. If

long hours take too much time away from the golf course — consider dermatology. The smooth operator will choose cardiology because as long as there are Princesses, Princes will continue to have heart failure.

## DENTIST

Another way to extract big bucks is for the Prince to sink his teeth into this profession. The rare dental emergency is usually not life threatening enough to pull the D.D.S. away from the tennis court, the opera or the dinner table. And a night time toothache has never been known to drag a Prince away from an amorous moment with his eager Princess.

## ORTHODONTIST

While drilling for oil can be lucrative for Blake or J.R., just drilling for cavities or designing dentures is often not rewarding enough for the Prince. A career in orthodontia can straighten out this guy's life for good.

## LAWYER

We don't mean to make a federal case out of this, but the son who really wants to do justice to his mother chooses a career in court. A trial provides a perfect stage for the Prince to perform, and gives him the audience he's always been craving.

## ADVERTISING EXECUTIVE

The Prince is taught to sell *himself* at an early age. He can put this skill to work pushing other people's products. It's a real pleasure trip to know that he's influencing the buying decisions of consumers everywhere. The hours are long, the ulcers are many, but an agency with *his* name on the door is enough to make his mother *kvell*.

## REAL ESTATE

Developer, Syndicator, General Partner. It's much more than just putting a roof over people's heads. The decrease in mortgage rates is directly proportionate with the increase in this Prince's portfolio.

## MOVIE MOGUL

From Samuel Goldwyn to Steven Spielberg, the talented Prince wants to see his name in lights. The chance to shmooze with celebs is irresistible. And a night at the Oscars provides a perfect place to see and be seen. What could be more gratifying than hearing the words "Thanks Mom" broadcast all across America.

## RETAILER

These purveyors of shoes, clothes, food and furs etc. are direct descendants of the push cart mavins on the lower east side. They've refined the methods of hawking wares to a fine art and have the *sheckels* to show for it.

## INVESTMENT COUNSELOR

Stock Broker, Banker, Certified Financial Planner. Telling other people what to do with their dough is somehow in the Prince's blood. He follows the market reports with religious zeal. This calculating Prince can often be found immersing himself in the *Wall Street Journal* or a scotch — but neither to excess.

## UNPRINCELY PROFESSIONS

**Astronaut**
**Fireman**
**Quarterback**
**Agribusinessman**
**Social Worker**
**Electrician**
**Gumshoe**
**Jockey**
**Locksmith (not loxsmith)**
**Interior Decorator**
**Maintenance Engineer**
**Priest**

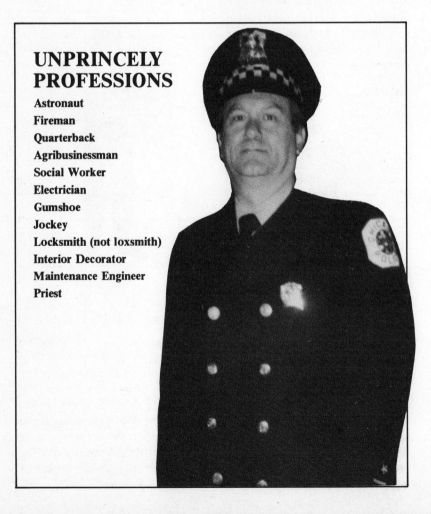

# ESSAY ON COMMODITIES BROKER

BUY! SELL! PUT! CALL! #$%¢&*@!!! Ah, the life of the commodity-trader Prince. To listen to these beleagured Princes tell it, you'd think they went to work in the coal mines. Gold mines is more like it.

True, they rise at dawn, then stand around packed like sardines, screaming at the top of their lungs, the sweat dripping. But that's where the similarity to the mines ends. For what coal miner has a $50 haircut, handkerchief linen shirt and Rolex watch?

Perhaps it would be better to compare the trading Prince to the lemmings. All sport the identical haircut, the identical clothes, watches and shoes. And they all drive the same car. If one trader goes out to buy a Jeep, you can be sure all his friends in the pit will be driving a Jeep before the month's end. Are they all following the same path to destruction? That all depends on who you talk to. All this keeping up with the Jacobses is expensive. But these guys can afford it. And they'll be happy to tell you.

They'll complain to anyone who will listen about how tough the commodities markets are. Yes, they'll certainly be glad to tell you their sob stories on the golf course, on their boat or in their hot tub — any afternoon of the week. They'll even tell you why they'd prefer to wear a suit everyday. Probably so they can spend even more money on a work wardrobe. But don't sell these NJBs short. They make excellent catches in the long term for the lucky Princess who will spend her future with him.

# HIGH HOLIDAY NETWORKING

Since the Prince only goes to temple three times a year, it is imperative that he make the most of these visits. It is an opportunity to rub elbows with all the Big *Machers* who congregate on the temple steps. The scene below took place last *Rosh Hashana* at temple Judea.

"So, Harry, business must be good. You pledged a bundle at the bond drive."

"Could be better. You know my sister is getting a divorce. Know anyone who specializes in taking *putzes* like the *schlemeil* she married to the cleaners?"

## Macher #1

**Clothing manufacturer. Net worth $750,000 (post-divorce).**

## Macher #2

**Stockbroker. Net worth depends on the market.**

**The Nether Side of Networking:** Business relationships aren't the only ones that get cemented at these High Holiday sidewalk conferences. Every Stuart, Mel and Normie has a sister, cousin, neice or daughter who is still unattached. Many a match has been inscribed in the book of life on this *Yom Tov*. For what better place is there to meet a *hamischer* guy who wants to spend an extra day in temple this year — getting married.

•id I hear my name? What do
u say we discuss this case over
ound of golf tomorrow if the
ather holds."

"Golf sounds great! Let me call the office and check my patient load. Should be light after the holidays."

## Macher #3

**Lawyer. Net worth $1,000,000 (post Macher #1's divorce).**

## Macher #4

**Plastic Surgeon. Net worth very high from adjusting gross incoming patients.**

# POWER BRUNCHING
## Dealing Over Deli

When the Prince needs to wrap up a deal, he does it over deli. When negotiating with his attorney, Nova is in order. And if he forgets to send a brokerage client a dividend check, his client may call him and query, "What am I, chopped liver?" To which the Prince replies, "No, and just to prove it, I'll even take you out to brunch: Lox, bagels, cream cheese — the whole *schmear*."

The Prince always thinks better on a full stomach, but he must always order the right foods that deliver the message he wants to send. To guarantee your deals are *kosher,* here's what's in order:

---

**Potato Latkes —**
Remind your opponent of *Hannukah*. Make him more generous with his *gelt*.

**Chicken Soup with Matzoh Balls —**
Never order this if you're a doctor. It may put you out of business. Otherwise, just don't dribble on your tie.

**Brisket —**
Shows that you mean business, no strings attached.

**Gefilte Fish —**
Real *Machers* don't eat Gefilte Fish.

**Bicarbonate of Soda —**
Served with cigars, make the perfect degoustif.

**Creamed Chipped Beef on Toast —**
Offer this when dining with your *goyish* clientele.

**Smoked fish platter —**
Don't be a *chazer*. When feeling magnanamous, order this and offer to share.

**Flanken in the pot (or any variation of *gedempte fleish*) —**
This hearty dish is appropriate for times when the upper hand is needed. It will remind your associate of his early days with Mama, and render him incapable of opposition. Be sure to say the *flanken* is not as good as Mother used to make.

**Fried Matzoh —**
Eat this when you want to show you're making a sacrifice.

**Corned beef or pastrami sandwhich —**
Add coleslaw and Russian dressing to convey a devil-may-care attitude. Better yet, order it on a Kaiser roll.

# CONTENTS OF THE ATTACHE
## The Inside Story

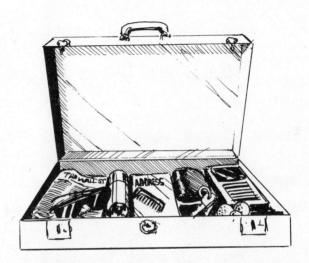

1. **Keys to the Porsche — 14K gold.** Even his significant other doesn't have a set.

2. **Watchman** — to catch sports scores and stock market reports.

3. **Calculator** — adds to his special self-image.

4. **Maalox** — the Prince's official post-prandial beverage — post-broker's meeting, post-alimony payment, post-pinochle, etc.

5. **Wall Street Journal** — the right read for commuters.

6. **Hair spray and comb** — for back combing after getting caught in a breeze.

7. **Wallet** — contains plastic, Wrestlemania tickets, business cards and a Jewish bankroll hundred dollar bill wrapped around singles.)

8. **Solid gold golf tees** — gift from old girlfriend.

9. **Monogrammed golf balls** — gift from ex-wife. Prince winces every time he uses them.

10. **File folders** — contain all important documents dealing with his latest case, acquisition or business plan.

11. **Airline tickets to Miami** — for upcoming business trip/golf weekend.

12. **Frequent flyer cards** — Princes unite to take advantage of free fare deals. (What, the Prince should pass up a bargain?)

13. **Porsche sunglasses** — makes the Prince feel sporty and macho, even behind the wheel of a 4-door Cadillac.

14. **Address book** — *guilt* edged and monogrammed.

## DIAL-A-GUILT TRIP #2

Prince: Hello?

Mother: Marky, is that you? You answer the phone while you're driving?

Prince: What do you expect? You called me on my car phone.

Mother: Well, I didn't mean you should answer in traffic. At least you should pull off the road.

Prince: Are you calling for a reason Mom?

Mother: Does a mother need a reason to call? *But* as long as I'm talking to you, your father and I have some papers for you, big shot lawyer, to look over.

Prince: Can it wait until next week? I'm working on an important case. In fact, I'm on my way to the airport right now to pick up the client.

Mother: Well, your father and I won't be around forever, you know . . . and neither will Patricia.

**Prince:** Mom, you're not talking about your will again, are you? You'll be here forever. They're not ready for your nagging *up there* yet. And who's Patricia?

**Mother:** That snotty sister-in-law of yours already has her eye on my silver. And you remember Patricia, Marcus, Ruthie's little girl.

**Prince:** Listen Mom, I'm already at the terminal, I have to go. I'll come for dinner next Friday night. But only if it's just you and Dad. I just remembered fatty Patty.

**Mother:** Okay mister big shot lawyer. Go see your fancy clients. Just remember who pushed you to go to law school.

**Prince:** How did I ever think this mobile phone was a great idea when you gave it to me for Hannukah?

# THE CREDIT CONNECTION

You may not recognize me but . . .

I buy my dress for success suits from my friends in the rag trade.

I own all the latest gadgetry (after all, if one is good, two is better.)

A Cadillac Seville is my favorite carriage.

My Rolex helps me keep track of my valuable time.

And I'm always welcome in the finest places.

*Credit.* **You can't be a Prince without it.**

# FAMOUS JEWISH PRINCES
## F.J.B. Honor Roll

F.J.B.'s (Famous Jewish Boys) have made great contributions to mankind in science, music, politics and the arts. But their greater contributions have been to womankind. Just think of all those *kvel-*ling Jewish mothers. For all those mamas past and present, here is a compendeum of those boys whose accomplishments are so great, they need no explanation.

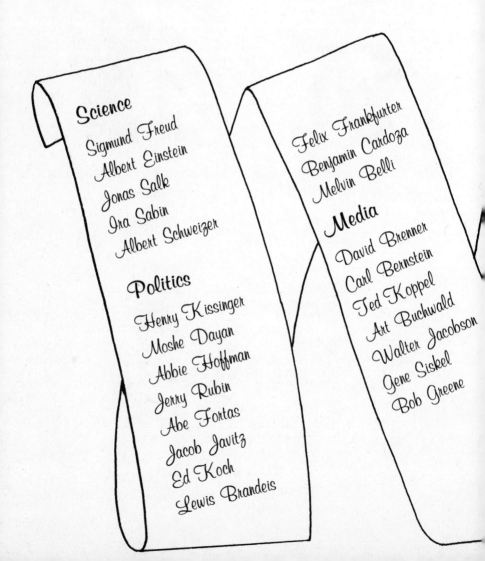

### Science

Sigmund Freud
Albert Einstein
Jonas Salk
Ira Sabin
Albert Schweizer

### Politics

Henry Kissinger
Moshe Dayan
Abbie Hoffman
Jerry Rubin
Abe Fortas
Jacob Javitz
Ed Koch
Lewis Brandeis

Felix Frankfurter
Benjamin Cardoza
Melvin Belli

### Media

David Brenner
Carl Bernstein
Ted Koppel
Art Buchwald
Walter Jacobson
Gene Siskel
Bob Greene

## Sports

Mark Spitz
Ken Holtzman
Sandy Kofax
Steve Grossman

## The Arts

Eddie Fisher
Marc Chagall
Steven Speilberg
Kirk Douglas
Paul Newman
Steve Allen
George Burns
David Birney
Howie Mandell
Richard Lewis
Judd Hirsch
Phillip Roth
Saul Bellow
Richard Benjamin
Peter Sellers
David Steinberg
Steven Gutenberg
Robert Klein

Alan Jay Toback
(cover Prince)

## Music

Bob Dylan
Irving Berlin
Ira Gershwin
Arthur Feidler
David Lee Roth
Oscar Hammerstein
Itzhak Perlman
Vladimir Horowitz
Alan Jay Lerner

## YOU DON'T HAVE TO BE JEWISH*

**Prince Charles**
**Prince Andrew**
**Prince Henry**
**Prince**
**John F. Kennedy**
**Bruce Springsteen**
**David Letterman**
**F. Lee Bailey**
**Johnny Carson**
**Ben Bradlee**
**Christian Barnard**
**Ray Strobel**

**\*To be a Prince**

# STAIRWAY TO HEAVEN
## Climbing the Corporate Ladder

Pity the poor Prince. His climb to the top isn't always as easy as it appears to be. There are many obstacles along the way. His boss (his father) simply cannot understand why he needs a corner office with a private shower. But how else can the Prince possibly freshen up for evening meetings with lovely lady clients.

The Prince has to work *months* before he can trade in his first company car for a Mercedes. And it isn't easy persuading the corporate accountant (his brother-in-law) that even a *clerk* on the company legal staff needs an expense account. How else can be escort Judge Friedman's daughter to the JUF ball? Indeed, how can he even be a JUF donor?

No one believes the Prince when he argues that a company yacht would be a successful image builder, or that they should charter a boat to the islands for the annual stockholders meeting. Never mind that all the stockholders are immediate family, it's still a great write-off.

The Prince has to pay his dues just like everyone else. And speaking of dues, what about that membership to Hillcrest?

So what if the Prince begins his climb to the top not at the bottom of the ladder, but halfway to the top. He'll have his neck wrung by his father, by his mother and by his wife if he isn't a fabulous success in the early days of his career. It isn't easy pleasing all those relatives. But it *is* only relative, because Princes always manage to be a *step up* on the competition.

# TERMS OF INVESTMENT
# A Prince of a Dictionary

How much is your net really worth? Use this handy glossary to define your money making abilities.

## Annuity:
The amount the Prince must guarantee to pay his girlfriend every year if she'll agree to become his wife. An amount more than he can ever hope to afford.

## Arbitrage:
The transaction involved in buying a suit on the lower east side and then trying to return it to Bloomingdale's.

## Bonds:
What the Prince is absolutely never able to break with his mother.

**C.D.:**
The size of the breasts every Prince hopes to get his hands on.

**Collateral:**
What the Prince's future father-in-law uses his business, as in convincing the Prince to marry his daughter.

### Return on investment:
The favors the Princess bestows on the Prince in direct proportion to how much he spends on her.

**Fannie Mae:**
What the Prince promises to name his first daughter if his Aunt Fannie will just lend him the down payment for his first house.

**Freddie Mac:**
Her ex-husband who the Prince threatens to name his first son after if Fannie won't come up with the down payment.

## Sallie Mae:
A risky investment because the Prince's daughter, Sallie, may not make it through Brandeis, the Prince's alma mater.

## Mutual Fund:
What the Princess considers the Prince's salary.

## IRA:
1) The Prince's accountant. They're always on a first name basis.

2) What the Prince will have to rely on in his old age based on the lousy advice his accountant has been giving him.

## Monetary velocity:
The speed at which the Princess spends every last dime the Prince earns.

## Platinum futures:
What life holds in store for the young Amex green card holder.

## Rollover:
The motion used by Princesses before they play dead when in bed with their husbands.

## NOW Checking:
Demanded by the Prince's son and daughter just before they leave for college.

## 401K:
The size of a Princess's engagement ring.

## Stocks:
Where the Prince will be tied and publically punished by his Princess if he doesn't invest their nest egg wisely.

## International Monetary Markets:
Expensive locals to be considered when planning a vacation. Not considered as safe as they used to be.

## Prospectus:
What the Prince must submit when asking for a Princess's hand in marriage.

## Limited partnership:
When the Prince does not turn over all his credit cards to his Princess.

## Tax shelter:
Vacation home in the Hamptons.

## Hostile takeover:
When the Prince steals his roommate's girlfriend, sticking him with an expensive rent when he leaves to go move in with her.

## Personal Banker:
What the Prince's wife and children consider him.

## Profit sharing:
What the Princess does with the Prince's income at every better department store in town.

# Chapter Six

# THE ROYAL PERSONA AND PHYSIQUE

## A Princely Profile

# PERSONALITY PROFILE
## The Royal Personna

"Whatever makes *you* happy."          "You'll see who's crazy . . ."

"Has anyone seen my Hush Puppies?"

### THE HAIMISHER PRINCE

This stay-at-home nice guy is the perfect catch for the less than social Princess. Makes a Killing at the office. Comes home asking for nothing more than a hot brisket dinner like his *Bubbe* used to make. Guys like the Haimisher Prince for his great sandwiches on poker night. Average looks, average body. Tends to fade onto the furniture he is always comfortably ensconced in.

### THE NEBISH PRINCE

The Revenge of the Nerds and Pee Wee Herman have made this *schlep* fashionable. Considers flood pants a fashion statement. Better at wooing mothers than Princesses. Every mother's dream, every Princess's nightmare. No discernible muscles whatsoever. Glasses instead of contacts . . . a dead giveaway.

### THE MESHUGGENEH

The wild man. Always coming up with some crazy scheme . . . whether it's for making money or meeting girls. Unmistakable insane gleam in his eyes. Beware of Princes wearing sunglasses. Bears remarkable resemblance to a mad scientist right down to the electric socket hairdo.

Princes come in all shapes and sizes. But no matter what they look like, all of their mothers think they have such a *shana punim*. Princes are usually easily distinguishable, but just in case there's any doubt . . .

"I hope your mom invites us back for Shabbas dinner next week . . . "

"Let me tell you what *I* think."

"What do you mean I'm insensitive?"

### THE MENSCH

Winner of the NJB popularity contest. Good looks, great job with income to match. Always a good provider, even if his Princess spends it faster than he makes it. Friends don't envy his success because he always shares it with them. Above average looks, but not intimidatingly so.

### THE SCHMUCK

Beneath heavy good *chi* and hairy chest lies a heart of solid stone. (Which also happens to be his mother's maiden name.) He's uniformly nasty to everyone. Mama Stone convinced him that he is God's gift to the universe. Nice Job Mama! Always expects everyone to be at his beck and call but never around when anyone else needs him.

### THE MAVIN

This know-it-all can always get it for you wholesale. Never lets you pick up the check . . . as he will always remind you. World's greatest authority on every subject. Thinks everybody is his best friend which is why no one can stand him. Big belly matches his big mouth.

# GETTING INTO SHAPE
## And Staying There

Great Princely bodies were made, not born. Jewish boys have two basic body types, neither of which has a base of muscles. After all, what can you expect from boys brought up on starch and *schmaltz?*

## The Fresser

The only exercise this Prince gets is lifting his fork to his mouth. Never even burns calories with a trip to the fridge because his Princess makes those trips for him. Speaking of trips, it's suspected that many of the fat cells in his body may have come over steerage with his Uncle Hymie from Kishnev who never needed an ox to pull his plow.

## The Vonce

Skin and bones, skin and bones! Mother claimed his baby picture looked like the skull and crossbones on the iodine bottle. Spent summer days wearing heavy sweaters because mom was afraid he'd catch his death of cold, and he already looked like death warmed over. This hyper Prince doesn't have an extra ounce of flesh anywhere. Except, of course, between his ears. Relies on brains rather than brawn.

# HAIR TODAY . . . GONE TOMORROW
## A Losing Battle

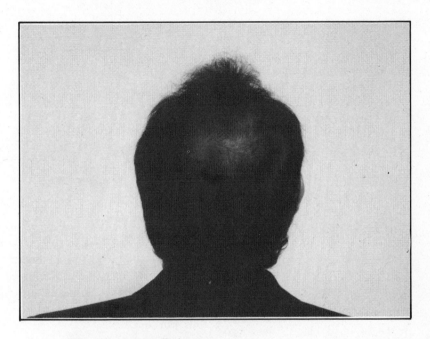

Pity the poor Prince,
His hair loss makes him wince.
The shininess of his pate,
Does nothing but make him irate.
When he combs long strands over the top,
His head resembles a mop.
And at the slightest breeze,
One side hangs down to his knees.
He can always get toupeed,
But it's a hassle when getting laid.
Instead of running fingers through his hair.
Princesses spend his money on things to wear.
But he doesn't let his hair loss stop him,
There's not a hirsuite guy to top him.

# THE PRINCELY WORKOUT

God did not favor Princes with muscular bodies. Instead he gave them enough money so they could join the best health club in town. For those Princes who want to take advantage of this opportunity (and keep the odds of early heart failure down to a minimum) there are a number of Princely Programs to follow. Each of these routines will help the Prince to improve his body and his image. And besides working out has become so fashionable that many Princes are trading a golf week in Miami for long weekends at swanky spas like La Costa.

But whether a weekend or a way of life, today's Princes must commit to be fit. And here's how to go about it . . .

**Weight Training:** Lifting your bankroll isn't enough. Don't be intimidated by the Mr. America types. In no time at all you'll be kicking sand in their faces.

**Aerobics:** Great for the cardio-vascular system and for meeting women wearing scanty leotards.

**Racquetball:** The fierce competition gives you a physical and psychological workout. Short shorts will show off a great tush. (best displayed for female opponents).

**Tennis:** You might not get into great shape, but you can sure show off your great sports wardrobe. Expensive racquet a must. And you can actually eat lunch before this workout.

**Nautilus:** Perfect for Princes who can't do anything for themselves. Machines that do all the work take the place of the women in your life.

**Swimming:** Acceptable since the advent of waterproof Walkmen. Listen to the stock reports while you get in shape.

**Running:** Picture your mother, girlfriend, wife or boss chasing after you and you'll be a sprinter in no time.

**Stationary Bicycle:** The only time in your life that you get the feeling that you're going nowhere fast.

# The SCHVITZ

A sauna in a modern comfortable and clean health club is no rival for an authentic schvitz. The ritual of getting all heated up and then dousing the body with ice cold water is likened by the Prince to an evening with his Princess (but even better because it all takes place in the air of comraderie with the boys).

The *schvitz* is populated by lots of old Jewish men sitting around in their *gottkies*. These guys give young princes something to look forward to. One look at them tells the fledgling *schvitzer* that the steambath is really for gaining peace of mind, *not* for improving the waistline. The cleansing effects of the *schvitz* are negated by the corned beef sandwich and schnapps the Prince devours at the end of the evening. If the steambath doesn't make him sweat, the garlic in the dill pickles ought to. It is not uncommon for Princes to *add* a few pounds on *schvitz* night.

# DRESSING FOR SUCCESS
## At Work, Play and Love

## WORK

Counted among the Prince's professional assets is his savvy sense of style, as you can see from the work clothes shown here.

**Business Suit:** Cardin, Armani, YSL or tailor made. Best suits the lawyer or banker.

**Lab Coat:** In white, blue or grey, this is the prescribed look for MDs and the like.

**Linen Jacket and slacks:** This slightly rumpled look conceals the razor sharp mind of the ad exec, movie mogul, or other creative Prince.

Clothes make the Prince. When they're made of natural fibers they also make him irristible to Princesses. Great tailoring can hide a multitude of sins. Pleated pants can camouflage a big pair of *poulkes*. Padded shoulders can change a slope-shouldered Prince into an illusion of a he-man. And shoes with a little lift can help lift the Prince's stature. Here is compendium of the styles that today's chic Princes are sporting.

# PLAY

It's hard to tell which the Prince enjoys more . . . dressing for the sport or actually playing it. Dare he disturb the line of his clothes by working up a sweat?

**Sweat Suit:** Filas and Ellesse are the names closest to the Prince's heart for looking good to and from the main event.

**Golf Outfit:** Golf shirt and pants should never shout you're a rival on the links but rather announce it quietly. Kelly green slacks with spouting whale pattern is absolutely not acceptable.

**Tennis Outfit:** Tennis whites are a great backdrop for gold jewelry. Yellow is good too, for touting your tan.

# LOVE

No matter how disinterested in clothes the Prince is, he'll never be able to interest a Princess unless he's dressed the right way.

**Tuxedo:** Black tie evening make seducing young maidens that much easier.

**Robe:** For finishing off a successful evening. The perfect attire for making breakfast for dates that last till dawn.

**Sweater and slacks:** The NJB's date uniform. Make sure they're natural fibers or you might naturally get ignored by genuine Jewish Princesses.

## The Anti-Prince

Believe it or not, there are Princes who deny their royal heritage. This denial comes after an expensive education at a liberal arts college. The rebel Prince turns his back on luxuries that most other Princes take for granted. Of course their mothers claim to still love them (and even send them handsome checks to tide them over) even though their sons' wild ways are killing them. Who would of thought their smiling Bar Mitzvah boy would become a two-bit biker — or worse?

## FORBIDDEN SUITS

| | | |
|---|---|---|
| Brooks Brothers | White duck pants | Hushpuppies |
| Jos. A. Banks | Seersucker suits | Bush jackets |
| Harris Tweed | Anything pink | Corduroy sports jackets |
| Wing Tips | Pipe | Timex |
| Top Siders | Beret | Slogan tee shirts |
| White Bucks | Imitation anything | Dago tees |
| Ties with birds | Leisure suits | Chains and leather |

# FELLA'S GUIDE TO FUR

Why should Princesses have all the fun? What better way to show off big bucks than by wearing something as ostentatious as a fur. So what if everyone thinks you're a *groiser knocker?* Another reason to sport a fur is to compensate for the lack of fur on top of your *keppie.* Of course, you could always just wear a fur hat, but why not look hot and go for the whole *megillah?* If you're not sure just what to wrap yourself in, here's some help . . .

**Sheepskin:** A compromise between fur and fabric. Makes men feel macho. Remember the Marlboro man (Maybe Princes would be macho if they were riding the range instead of riding roughshod in their Sevilles).

**Beaver:** What Prince wouldn't want to immerse himself in this?

**Coyote:** The wily Prince will look luxurious in this skin.

**Mink:** For the frisky prince.

**Muskrat:** For parkas only. Fox trim is a sly way to say you've arrived.

**Raccoon:** For the sporty Prince. Make a statement at the stadium on cold or not so cold days.

# The Crown Jewels

Carrying around a big bankroll with a sterling silver money clip isn't enough for the Prince. Ideally, he'd like to hang his gelt around his neck, but in lieu of that he gilds himself with gold. And a diamond or two couldn't *hoit* either.

**Gold Chi:** In case there is any doubt of the wearer's affiliation. Looks best nestled in chest hair.

**Diamond Pinky Ring:** for the *alta cocker.*

**Mezzuzah:** for the adolescent Prince.

**Gold Chains:** Jewish dog tags.

**Gold ID Bracelet:** best with name in diamonds.

**Rolex:** so everyone knows how much your watch cost.

**Wedding Band:** to be worn either around the finger or through the nose.

**Diamond Tuxedo Studs:** a carat each will do. Cubic zirconia won't.

**Big Gold Cuff Links:** the bigger the better, especially with gem stones in them.

---

# FORBIDDEN FRUITS

Maltese cross
twist-o-flex watchband
collar pin
American Flag tie clip
String tie with Navaho slide clip

# Chapter Seven

# *Chi*
# SOCIETY

# The Social Prince

# THE RIGHT ADDRESS

Now that the Prince is out of college and advancing in the right career, it's time for him to find a place of his own and shift his social life into high gear.

The right address will guarantee his entry into the right social circles. (And soon Princesses will have him running around in circles as well.)

Princes choose places that are a complete contrast to the suburban palaces in which they grew up. There are several other guidelines the Prince uses when striking out on his own:

1. Always choose a big city over a small town. While the job opportunities in Muskeegee might bring in the big bucks, what good is being a big fish in a small pond if the highlight on your social season is at the local church ice cream social?

2. Choose an apartment in an elevator building *with* a doorman. These buildings are almost entirely inhabited by single women. Go directly to the laundry room. You'd be surprised at what a turn-on women begging to do your laundry can be.

3. Choose an apartment in a walk-up building *without* a doorman. There's no one to keep an eye on your comings and goings. And burglar bars are ever so much more macho than levelors.

4. Don't be embarrassed if all you can afford is a studio apartment.

You can always say that you're saving your money to start your own business.

5. If a two bedroom flat would leave you flat broke, a roommate is perfectly acceptable. Make sure he's no competition for your social life. It's best to choose a roommate with a girlfriend, especially one that can cook (and preferably one with her own apartment.)

## Where to Live: An Urban Example

**Chicago:** Lincoln Park, Gold Coast, SuHu
Three dry cleaners and two carry out spots per block. Even more BMWs. Look for ladies laying in the sun in the park and at Oak Street beach.

**Los Angeles:** Westwood, Santa Monica, Marina Del Rey
Look for bronzed goddesses at the private beaches in Malibu.

**Miami:** Coconut Grove, Coral Gables
The city never sleeps for those of you into vices. Take our advice and stay clean-shaven.

**New York:** Upper East Side, Upper West Side, The Village, SoHo, etc.
The city is teeming with Yuppies. Don't look for love in the summer in the city. Everyone leaves as the mercury rises.

**Washington, D.C.:** Georgetown, Capitol Hill
Clydes and Bars on M Street should govern your social life.

### Dial a Guilt Trip #3

**Prince:** Hi! I'm tied up and can't answer the phone right now, but I'd love to get back to you. So why don't you leave your name and number at the sound of the beep. Take it easy, but take it.

**Girlfriend:** Hello Bradley you schmuck. I know you're home. Who're you *shtuping* tonight? I'll bet *you're* not the one that's tied up. If you think that . . . (click)

**Prince:** Hi! I'm tied up and can't answer the phone right now, but I'd love to get back to you. So why don't you leave your name and number at the sound of the beep. Take it easy, but take it.

**Girlfriend:** I hate this machine! If you think that I'm ever going to speak to you again, you're sadly mistaken. I wouldn't go out with you again if you were the last man on earth! If you're not man enough to talk to me yourself, . . . (click)

**Girlfriend:** Hi! This is Lisa, I'm doing my nails right now and don't want to smear them by picking up the phone. Give me time to put on my top coat and I'll get back to you. Ciao!

**Prince:** Lisa — I just got *your* message. Do you want to come over for a pizza? You can pick it up on your way over. The pizza joint is right next to the bus stop. Don't forget the soda. See you at 8:00.

**Prince:** Hi! I'm tied up and can't answer the phone right now, but I'd love to get back to you. So why don't you leave your name and number at the sound of the beep. Take it easy, but take it.

**Girlfriend:** If you think I'm running over *with* a pizza . . .!

See you in an hour!

# THE PRINCE'S PAD
## The Royal Toy Box

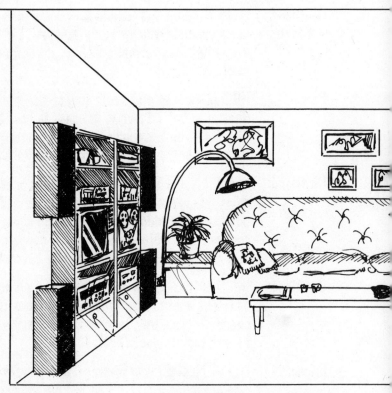

**Living Room**

1. Sofa and chairs — inherited when mother redecorated her living room. The first time the Prince has felt fabric rather than plastic.

2. Coffee table — purchased second-hand. Fortunately not visible under two-inch veneer of dust.

3. Entertainment Center — completely obscured by equipment! 26″ remote control stereo component color T.V., VCR with wireless remote, Laser disc player, Luxman receiver, Yamaha turntable, Sony reel-to-reel, AIWA cassette player, and four JBL speakers.

4. Indian Print Cushions — for extra seating. Everyone is forever picking out seeds.

5. Cordless telephone. Little Black Book.

6. Answering machine — contains permanent message from mother.

7. Bookcase — left over from college dorm room. Contains Black's Law Dictionary, The One-Minute Manager, Power Lunching, The Jewish American Princess Handbook, In Search of Excellence, back issues of Nation,

Finally able to afford the finer things in life, the Techno-Prince surrounds himself with all the latest gadgets. From his command module — a comfortable armchair — he can amuse himself for hours on end. At arms reach are the controls to his entertainment center, from compact disc player to VCR. The only thing the Prince can't remotely control is his Princess, but that's another story altogether!

Rolling Stone and Stereo Review, Ken Follet thrillers and the complete works of Xaviera Hollander.

8. Art: Framed posters of Superbowl XX, enlargements of photos from cross-country trip with college roommate, LeRoy Neiman prints and Big Ten Girls Calendar.

9. Tree lamp — housewarming present from Grandmother.

10. Carpet remnant — in color that clashes with sofa.

11. Ash tray — stolen from the Golden Nugget in Las Vegas.

12. Bamboo shades — do *not* keep light from entering.

13. Bar — fully stocked with Stoly, Tanqueray, Johnny Walker Black, Jameson's Irish Whiskey, Pimm's Cup, Jack Daniels, Bailey's Irish Cream, Kahlua, Amaretto and California Cooler. (Note: All bottles are sealed with the exception of Kahlua.) Certificate for Bordeaux futures hung above bar. Monogrammed highball glasses (usher's gift from best friend's wedding.)

14. Philadendron — in its final stages.

## Bedroom

16. King sized bed with earth tone velour comforter.

17. Mock-bearskin rug for this mock-macho man.

18. Night-table with candle, reading lamp with AM/FM clock radio. Inside drawer: Trojans, rolling paper, matches and hidden Playboys (old habits are hard to break), Little Black Book for something to occupy his hand during long, lonely nights.

19. Second set of Stereo Speakers — for serenading seductions.

20. Picture of Nude hanging above bed for inspiration.

21. Desk — Calculator, small T.V, Cross Bar Mitzvah Pen and Pencil set, name plate from last job, un-opened briefcase, Little Black Book II, application to Shalom Singles, desk lamp with halogen bulb (gift from last lover).

22. Closet — 25 White Shirts, 6 each of blue, beige, pink, cream and yellow. (Stripes are not Jappy.) 10 wearable suits — 3 of them double breasted. 10 non-wearable suits — *totally* out of fashion. ONE PAIR of dress shoes, six pairs of sneakers.

23. Hidden drug paraphernlia-can you identify the stash box in this picture?

24. Dresser — covered with keys, loose change, lava lamp.

25. Jewelry box — filled with collar stays.

26. Bamboo Blinds — to carry through the decorative motif from the living room.

## Bathroom

**27. Threadbare Terry Cloth Robe —** to wear for solo showers only.

**28. Plush Velour Robe —** to wear apres shower with date that lasts until morning.

**29. After shave —** at least 12 different bottles. None purchased personally by the Prince.

**30. Clinique Men's Skin System —** gift from Prince's sister. Used only by the Prince's girlfriend.

**31. Spare Toothbrushes and Disposable Razors —** God forbid a date should think of using *his*.

**32. Shampoo and Blow Dryer —** use on gentle for the perfect coif.

**33. Shower Tunes —** purchased when last date got electrocuted.

**34. See Through Shower Curtain —** designed to look like Massage Parlor Window.

**35. Set of Non-Matching Rough Towels —** some still have camp name tags, others say Holiday Inn on them.

**36. Reading Material —** *Forbes, Business Week, People, Time, Penthouse.*

**37. Three Way Mirror —** to aid in styling hair for proper coverage of bald spot.

**38. Tenax —** for the wet look. The 80's answer to Brill Cream.

**39. Little Black Book III —** when shower alone becomes too lonely.

**40. Brown Throw Rug —** a hideaway for hair balls.

**41. Permanently overflowing laundry basket —** with month's supply of jockeys.

# WHY BLONDES
# GO FOR BOYCHICKS

"He Always Treats Me Great.
Gosh . . . I Mean Like a . . . Princess!"

"Mamas don't let your girls grow up to be housewives . . . " All wily mothers, Jewish and Gentile alike, agree that Jewish boys make the best marriage material. Generations of Jewish moms have taught their sons to love, honor and, above all, *obey* the whims of their women.

Lucky ladies who can land a Prince will never have to lift a finger around the house (that is except to put on her diamonds.) Jewish boys are completely convinced that maids are a religious tradition. Without help in the house, how could any woman carry out her duties of attending fashion shows, going to luncheons and shopping?

What's more, Princes do *not* have blue collar jobs. They even go to the office on weekends. No sitting around the house in their under-shirts watching T.V., guzzling beer and packing down ham sandwiches for *these* top caliber catches.

And a Prince would sooner beat a path to the grocery store than beat his wife for not having grub on the table.

Another reason that Jewish guys are such gems is that they shower their brides with diamonds, rubies and emeralds rather than vacuum cleaners, toasters and fishing equipment. Princes take their wives on trips to the Caribbean and teach them how to snorkel. Gentile men take their wives camping and teach them how to scale fish.

Even if the Prep Princess converts, her mother-in-law will continue to refer to her as *the shikse* and keep her at arms length (However this distance can be considered a blessing.)

Other advantages the Prince can offer are a home in the suburbs rather than a trailer park, a Porsche instead of a pick-up, weekly trips to the beauty shop instead of the butcher shop, trips to Monte Carlo instead of to the local bingo parlor and the use of an interior decorator instead of an order form from the Sears Catalog.

Yes, it's obvious the Prince is a great catch. And the best part of marrying a prince is that there is no man who can catch up to him.

# WHY DAVIDS DESIRE DEBS

## Forbidden Fruit

Not to belabor a point, but Nice Jewish Boys just can't resist the allure of natural blonde hair, blue eyes, a God given upturned nose and a mouth that doesn't issue forth constant complaints. Does this dream dish really exist? You bet, but she's certainly not the girl next door!

To meet his fantasy girl, the Prince must frequent Polo matches and Yachting Races. A weekend at the Cape couldn't hurt either.

Once the Prince makes contact, where does he take these young debs for a date? Somewhere where all his friends can see him, no doubt. No matter that his date sticks out like a sore thumb with her lack of make-up and simple but elegant pony tail (Of course, Muffy's a must as a moniker). And could this bashful beauty really drink the Prince under the table? Of course. While the Prince sips a cranberry juice cocktail, she'll be knocking back Cape Codders like there's no tomorrow.

What else is it about wonder bread that captivates the Prince? One grope will tell you. No fuss, no muss. She remains the picture of buttoned-down respectability even with the Prince pawing at her pearls. And unlike a Princess, she genuinely enjoys this wild romp. It hearkens back to fond memories of the days of her youth, when touch football games with her brother's prep school chums brought her her first encounters.

This wasp princess appeals because she's just as happy eating beer nuts at the corner tavern as she is dining on lobster at Tavern on the Green. She'd be just as game to watch the Mets as to attend the Metropolitan Opera. And a bunch of daisies will get the Prince farther with her than furs and jewels will with a Jap.

What's more, he never has to meet her clan, and his mother would *cholish* if he brought her home to dinner. But better he should get dating *shickses* out of his system early, before it's too late because he could never alter his life enough to take one of these forbidden fruits to the altar.

# IF IT'S NOT BROKEN, DON'T FIX IT (UP)
## "Have I Got A Girl For You!"

It's an age old tradition to fix up Jewish Princes with *Nice Jewish Girls*. Young or old, there's a *yente* in everyone's life. No matter how satisfied the Prince is with his present social status, no one is willing to leave well enough alone. The temptation to fix him up is just too great.

Is he short or tall? Fat or thin? Rich or Poor? None of this seems to matter. The fact that he is a male is enough. That's why Lois Marmelstein, who tips the scales at 180 lbs. and stands 5′ 11″ in her stocking feet, was seen last Saturday with Sherwin Cohen whose nickname is Half-Pint and who is a borderline anorexic.

It is also why Sandra Perelmuter, Assistant Curator at the Met, was matched up with Larry Lazaar, who hasn't missed a Knicks, Rangers, Yankees, Islanders or Mets game or boxing match at the Garden since 1966.

These kind of (miss) matches continue to be arranged every day because they're not *all* misguided. Some of them do work out which is why the Prince continues to go on blind dates anyway.

Of course he does exercise caution when selecting where to take these

dates. It's a good idea to pick out three or four different places to go. If she's a double-bagger, he'll take her to a movie, get there right as the coming attractions are starting, buy her her own box of popcorn and plead a headache so they can slip out unnoticed before the show ends.

If she's a knockout, he'll knock himself out and take her someplace that will dazzle her *and* dazzle any of his friends that happen to see them.

When the long-awaited or far-too-early end of the evening rolls around, the Prince has several options. If he never wants to see her again, he'll mumble something

about having a nice time and say he'll call her. If all systems are go, he will invite himself in to her apartment. Should she decline that invitation, he will ask her to brunch the next day.

No matter what the outcome of the date, the Prince is usually pretty happy to be back home safe and sound. As his post-date ritual, he collapses onto the couch and turns on his answering machine and gets the message, " . . . have I got a girl for you . . . " And so it goes!

## When Once is Enough

My sister had been trying to fix me up with a friend of hers from work. Finally, I gave in and made a date with Hillary. We had a nice time, but no big deal. During the course of the evening, she met my roommate Mitch. Unbeknownst to me, Mitch got her phone number and they quietly began dating. Once I found out, Hillary started looking a lot more enticing. So I called her again, just to talk. One call led to another. Soon Mitch was out of the picture, and Hillary and I were in one — our wedding portrait. I think Mitch knew what would happen all along. But what are friends for anyway?

*Bobby Finerman*

# The Booze to choose

During the Prince's formative years, mama brought out the Manischewitz only on the holidays. And if it was a really important occasion, for example, the Prince's *Bris,* the men might take a sip of schnapps.

It's no wonder the Prince is no shikker. No hoisting the brewskies for our Prince.

But gaining an appreciation for liquid libation is a must for the modern Prince. So in case you haven't cultivated a taste for the fruit of the vine, here's a few tipsy tips — *L'chaim!*

## CHAMPAGNE
Be sure to order Brut. (No that's not the cologne you wore at your Bar Mitzvah.) Also the basis for a Kir Royale and a mimosa.

## CAMPARI
Better to order this for your date instead. You may not look pretty in pink.

## DAQUIRI
Princes love blender drinks. Always ask if the fruit is fresh.

## KAHLUA
Princes think that White Russians are a macho drink. Maybe it's a throwback to their peasant ancestors.

## AMARETTO
The way to make your Princess amorous. Best when served with cream to take the edge off this potent potable.

## COGNAC
Don't bother with a snifter, the Prince uses this as a cure for the sniffles.

## WINE
Princes drink white with everything. Even when the Prince drops words like oaky, insouciant, amusing, impertinent and pretentious he still always orders a carafe of the house brand.

## VODKA
Choose an expensive import on the rocks. Ordered widely by Princes because it has little or no taste. Stolie, Absolute, Finlandia.

## SCOTCH
An acquired taste most often tasted at business dinners. Order Dewars with soda and a twist, hard to differentiate from a white wine spritzer.

## LONG ISLAND ICED TEA
For Princes looking to get really shnookered. Five kinds of liquor cunningly disguised to appeal to the Prince's sweet tooth.

# HOW TO DATE BIMBOS WITHOUT LOSING YOUR

## Upwardly Mobile Princely Heritage

**Guest Editorial by
Steve Lakowitz
Myron Goldstin**

Purely for puriant reasons, the Prince pursues these luscious ladies who will satisfy fantasies he's had since his first Playboy in his underwear drawer. While these women will respond to his every sexual whim he must be cautious about giving in to the desire to date these dollies. What an embarrassment for friends and family!

If the allure is too strong, however, and he cannot resist, he must know how to operate. So here is a definition of these dishes . . . how to meet them and what to do with them.

**Bimbos: a definition**
Females possessing two or more of the following:
1. Farah Fawcett hairdo
2. Membership in a Tanning Salon
3. Beautician's License
4. Charge Account at Casual Corner
5. Portfolio of nude Polaroids to be submitted to Playboy
6. Bottle of Charlie or Musk cologne in purse
7. Imitation Louis Vuitton bag
8. Flight attendant application
9. The desire to be a model or an actress
10. Experience as a cocktail waitress

**Bimbo meeting places**
1. Wet T-Shirt or tight jean contest
2. Professional sports cheerleader tryouts
3. Convention booths
4. Acting Classes
5. Ladies Night Happy Hours
6. Stock car races

**Where to take a Bimbo to eat**
1. Any Wags, Howard Johnson's or Stuckey's
2. All drive through restaurants
3. Tollways
4. Room Service
5. Any place 90 minutes or more from your home
6. Any place with a salad bar
7. Her apartment

## Where *not* to take a Bimbo to eat
1. Your Mother's House
2. Any restaurant where place setting has more than one fork
3. Anywhere you'll be known by your first name
4. Anywhere you'd like to return to
5. Your sister's machetenum
6. Your apartment

## Where to entertain a Bimbo
1. Any Playboy Club
2. Drive-In Movie
3. Wrestling Matches
4. Hotel Discos
5. Any dinner playhouse featuring Van Johnson
6. Auto Shows
7. Her apartment

## Where *not* to entertain a Bimbo
1. Your mother's house
2. Your apartment
3. High school, college or grad school reunion
4. Friend's and family wedding
5. A Passover, seder or bris
6. Your office (during office hours.)
7. Anywhere you have season tickets
8. Your apartment

## Where to vacation with a Bimbo
1. Downtown Las Vegas
2. Jamaica in July or Acapulco in August
3. Anywhere in Indiana
4. Atlantic City
5. Anyplace in a Winnebago
6. Her apartment

## Where not to vacation with a Bimbo
1. A business convention or seminar with colleagues
2. Your parent's condo in Miami
3. A wedding chapel in Las Vegas
4. Any posh spa like La Costa
5. Any place in season
6. Israel

## What to talk about with a Bimbo
1. Your car
2. Your profession
3. Recent article in Cosmo
4. Her modelling or acting aspirations
5. Kinky sex
6. Why you're so quiet
7. Birth Control
8. Her apartment

## What *not* to talk about with a Bimbo
1. Living together
2. Commitments
3. Ring Sizes
4. Converting
5. Children
6. Your mother

## How to get rid of a Bimbo
1. Tell her you've had a vasectomy
2. Tell her you've turned gay
3. Have your mother call her
4. Turn her over to your Uncle Shermy
5. Tell her you lied about being Jewish

# AFTER HOURS AVAILABILITY
## A Guide to Metropolitan Nightlife

## MIAMI

**MONDAY — Pumpernicks**
Redeem yourself after a hell raising weekend by taking your *bubbe* out to dinner. Enjoy corned beef and don't forget to take home the rolls.

**TUESDAY — Federation Dances**
The perfect place to pick up a princess. See your past pass before your eyes. Rekindle an old romance or two.

**WEDNESDAY — CATS**
For Princes on the prowl. Find a friendly feline type and have a wild evening.

**THURSDAY — The Parallel Bar and Body Centre**
Make sure your social life works out at this new hotspot. Feel in the pink and mint a new romance.

**FRIDAY — Biscayne Baby**
Drink, dance, lose yourself in Wild Romance. Go on Friday nights — heat up the rest of your weekend.

**SATURDAY — The Keys**
A weekend here with your friends and lover could be the key to a promising future.

**SUNDAY — Backyard Barbeques**
Find a friend with a pool out back. And don't back out of meeting a tanned beauty he's good friends with.

## LOS ANGELES

**MONDAY — Stay home** and work out with your personal trainer. Your fitness goal is to make sure *she's* blonde, blue-eyed and stacked.

**TUESDAY — Voila in Beverly Center**
After an appointment at Bijan, make an appointment to have drinks with your current main squeeze at this trendy food factory.

**WEDNESDAY — Spago**
A business dinner at this Hollywood hot spot can turn into an evening to satisfy your other appetites.

**THURSDAY — Tramps, Pips**
Join the swank set at these private establishments, and establish yourself as a desirable catch for west coast women.

**FRIDAY — Helena's**
The newest stop on the social circuit. You'll be high on life at heavenly Helena's.

**SATURDAY — Malibu**
Seek sun and fun on the private beaches. Busy yourself with the best beach bunnies. Find a friend with a yacht and head for the marina.

**SUNDAY — Hard Rock Cafe**
Eat to the Beat. Or maybe a poolside party is more your style.

# NEW YORK

**MONDAY — The Vertical Club**
Get in shape for the big week that's on your horizon. Meet your match on court and off.

**TUESDAY — America**
For a glorious social life, head for the bar at the back. You'll have stars in your eyes for all the gorgeous girls.

**WEDNESDAY — Odeon**
Take a wonderful woman for a chic meal at this downtown eatery. Park your limo right out front

**THURSDAY — Palladium**
Everyone who's anyone dances till dawn at the latest dance emporium favored by the beautiful people.

**FRIDAY — Memphis**
Where the yup pups eat, drink and make merry. Satisfy your craving for All American Cooking and All American Girls.

**SATURDAY — Hamptons; Fire Island**. Summer annex to the night spots above. Sun tan de rigeur. Sip your share of long island ice tea and blue whales.

**SUNDAY — Soho and Share Parties (Winter). L.I.E. & Midtown Tunnel (Summer).**
From September to May, wander around the galleries and shops on West Broadway. Take time out to hit a share party or two to firm up your summer social scene. From June to August, spend late evenings heading back to the city. See and be seen in the right rented japmobile.

# CHICAGO

**MONDAY — East Bank Club**
After wild weekends of body abuse get back in shape at this posh city club. Give yourself a leg up on next weekend.

**TUESDAY — P.J. Clarke's**
For the afterwork crowd. Briefcase is the ultimate status symbol. Meet professional Princess who can afford to take *you* upstairs to dinner, instead of the cleaners.

**WEDNESDAY — Ultimate Sports Bar & Grill**
Shoot baskets and shoot the breeze with blonde haired ladies. Step into the ring with sportsminded girls.

**THURSDAY — Hunt Club & Gamekeepers**
Trot back and forth between these two hot spots. Stalk her at the Hunt Club. Bag her at Gamekeepers.

**FRIDAY NITE — Dixie Bar & Grill**
Good place to take bimbettes. Too noisy for conversation. Or get jazzed over a new conquest, then buy her dinner to start a spicy evening.

**SATURDAY NITE — Park West Video Dance Party or Clubland**
For the Partying Prince. Looking great in the latest fashion fads a must. Purple hair wouldn't hurt either.

**SUNDAY — Belden Deli and Nookies, Too!**
Yup! This is for Brunch! Don't be late if you had a hot Saturday night date.

# JAP MOBILES:
# The Royal Carriage

A classy car puts the Prince into high gear. He gets behind the wheel, puts on his shades, pops in a tape and leaves the real world far behind. His car of choice must be sleek, shiny and expensive. It should also reflect the driver's image, not only by being impeccably clean but by being so fast that it leaves everyone else biting his dust.

## Vanity Plates

| | | | |
|---|---|---|---|
| Y I WRK | J BOY | BABY DOC | MITZVAH |
| PRINCE | BOY CHX | STIR UP | NJB |
| JAP | I M RICH | 4 CEPS | NOSE JOB |
| KEPPI | BIG BUX | SNORT 1 | JUSTUS |
| BAGEL | I SUE 4 U | TAX JD | |

| WHAT'S HOT | WHAT'S NOT |
|---|---|
| **Porsche, Mazerati, Ferrari, Avanti, Corvette**<br><br>These cars are fast and flashy, despite the fact that the Prince has to get an automatic transmission. But he can't do anything for himself can he? | **Woody Le Barron Convertible, Dodge Dart, Cougar**<br><br>These will be a real standout in the bowling alley parking lot. |
| **BMW, Mercedes, Jaguar**<br><br>The stately sedans state that the Prince is solid but not stodgy. | **Country Squire Wagon, Ford Fairlane, Winnebago**<br><br>Great for tail gate parties. Plenty of room for the deviled eggs, spam mold and apple cider. |
| **Audi, Volvo, Saab**<br><br>These Yupmobiles feature a Yup Pup car seat as standard equipment. Sales are booming since the baby boomlet. | **Chevy Van, Isuzu Flatbed Truck, Nissan Hard Bodies**<br><br>Pile in the dogs, the kids, the kegs and a picnic basket and away you go. |
| **Cadillac, Buick, Oldsmobile**<br><br>These Jew canoes are favorite middle-aged status symbols. Always have 4-doors. So much fun playing with the electric door locks. | **Chevy, Chrysler, Ford**<br><br>Favorite middle-of-the-road roadsters. Look best hauling U-Haul. |

# NOUVELLE DATING
## More For Less

Nowadays dating isn't easy. In the past, one used to be able to take a Princess for a simple dinner and a show. In the 80's, the same date has evolved into dinner at a trendy restaurant serving small portions at big prices followed by a first-run play on Broadway. In the old days, this standard date was followed by a make-out session in the Princess's driveway. Today, the date often ends in a solo taxi ride from the restaurant. Is it any wonder then, why there is much confusion when it comes to dating practices?

| WHAT THE PRINCE SAYS | WHAT THE PRINCESS THINKS |
|---|---|
| Would you like to go out Saturday night? | Yes! (Not with you. But it is better than just washing my hair). |
| I think it would be fun to go to Chinatown for Chinese food. | A big spender! I bet he wants to take the subway. I'll definitely order lobster Cantonese. |
| Would you like to come up for a drink? | Doesn't he have a more original line than that? Should I ask to see his etchings? |
| I just moved into this building, and I don't know where the laundry room is yet. | Now he wants me to do his laundry. Who does he think I am, his mother? |
| Do you know how to make a great dinner? | Yes, I pick up the phone and order. |
| I got Wrestlemania tickets. | It beats wrestling with him all evening! |
| I had a great time tonight. I can't believe it was only our first date. | I'd better call my uncle the Jeweler, God willing. |

# THE PERFECT PRINCESS

The Perfect Princess is a myth created by Jewish Mothers. (Perfect Prima Donna would be a more apt moniker.) The Prince has a sixth sense for spotting Princesses. Until the time he's ready to be hooked, he usually has enough sense to run in the other direction when he spots one.

And, what is it that gives these NJG's away? Their uniformly "sunstreaked" hair? Their identical pert upturned noses (All designed by the same Master Sculptor . . . with a Park Avenue address)? Their perfectly manicured nails that have never touched a vacuum or a "hose"? Perhaps it's their magnetic personalities? They're attracted to anything that's expensive and ostentatious (which is why they're so attracted to Princes). Maybe it's that somehow familiar gleam in their eyes the Prince has seen somewhere before. Where? In the eyes of his mother.

The Prince is powerless to suppress this fatal attraction. After all, wasn't it good enough for his father and his *zayde?* Had they not succumbed where would the Prince be today? Maybe pumping gas on the interstate insted of pumping the hand of his partner after each successful business deal. And besides, what would happen if Princes didn't marry Princesses? Where would the world be if there were *no more* Jewish Mothers?

# Chapter Eight

# THE PRINCE AS KING?

## The Queen Rules the Roost

# It's Time for a Prince to Get Married When . . .

> **Doctor:** I'm sorry, but you only have 6 months to live.
> **Prince:** What do I do, Doc?
> **Doctor:** Move to Nebraska and marry a Jewish Princess. It'll be the longest 6 months of your life.

- He finds himself eagerly taking his mother up on her offers to fix him up.
- He's the last of his friends to be doing his own laundry.
- His friends are having their second children, and the girls he's dating are children themselves.
- He has a dish named for him at the Chinese take-out.
- He has a burning desire to take the same girl out more than once.
- He considers giving up his Sunday morning golf game with the guys, for Sunday morning brunch in bed with his girlfriend.
- He doesn't want to be totally bald in his wedding pictures.
- He's the only one who still shows up to meet "all the guys" at the bar on Friday nights.
- He is jealous when the guys sit around complaining about their wives.
- He and his eccentric bachelor Uncle Fred are beginning to be mentioned in the same sentence.
- He needs the tax advantage of owning a home, but doesn't have the advantage of having someone to share it with.
- He's sick of organizing everyone *else's* bachelor parties, and realizes it's time he had one of his own.
- His watch is broken and he's been eyeing a new Rolex.

# How to Spot a Perfect Princess

1. She offers to cook you dinner on your second date . . . your mother's homemade brisket recipe, no less.

2. She's eager for you to meet her family . . . especially her Uncle Maury, the diamond broker.

3. She never looks at other men when you're out taking romantic strolls in the city . . . she's too busy looking at the new spring fashions in all the shop windows.

4. She offers to pick up your clothes at the dry cleaners . . . her opportunity to check out the fabric content of your wardrobe.

5. She has a fantastic, high-paying job in her chosen field . . . which she is willing to *sacrifice* the minute you pop the question.

6. She takes an immediate liking to all your friends . . . they make excellent fodder for set-ups for all *her* girlfriends.

# ROMANCING THE STONE
## Wheeling and Dealing for Diamonds

Once the Prince has resigned himself to his fate of marrying a Princess, he knows he must give her a rock befitting her new status. Depending on *his* status, he acquires this gem (the ring that is) in one of several ways.

### All in the Family

The Princess is honored and flattered to be presented with an heirloom that was worn by the Prince's beloved grandmother. She is so overcome, that the first thing she does is go over to her uncle's jewelry store to have it appraised and reset.

### Going for Broke

What's lacking in romance can be made up for in stone size when visiting the dingy abode of the diamond broker.

These little old men know how to walk the fine line between making the Princess happy with her rock, but pricing it so it won't send the Prince into shock.

### Uncle Morris

The easy way out for the Prince. If the girl he gets has a family in the jewelry business, she'll have a rock in mind from her Bat Mitzvah day on.

### I Can Get It for You Retail

The least popular method for procuring the ring, and justifiably so. If getting engaged doesn't make the Prince nervous enough, paying full price certainly will.

---

## Princely Proposals

| He Pops the Question | She Replies |
|---|---|
| 1. In an expensive restaurant over a romantic candlelit dinner. | Yes, with no reservations. |
| 2. Spur of the moment proposal. | Yes! Thank God he didn't pick out the ring yet. |
| 3. After a hectic weekend with his kids. | Yes! I think boarding school is a wonderful experience. |
| 4. Before her younger sister's wedding. | Yes! Now she'll be able to go to the wedding with a date no less. |
| 5. On a Carribean beach during vacation. | Yes! A man with a tan. |
| 6. When your Sunday morning lox box turns out to have a ring inside. | Yes! She's always wanted a man who can cook. |

# SETTING UP THE SCHLEMIEL
## (In Her Father's Business)

There's one last chance for Princes who haven't made something of themselves. While not in and of itself a reason to get married, finding a Princess whose doting daddy owns a successful business certainly sweetens the pot. Meeting a Princess who's M.D. father has a thriving practice can be just the remedy for the resident who graduates at the bottom of his class. Finding a Princess whose father needs a flunky at his home decorating store will be perfect for the jobless Prince who feels like he's painting himself into a corner.

Even though he's been handed his job on a silver platter, the Prince will usually try to convince his father-in-law he's made a sterling investment in his daughter's future.

The Prince's grandiose ideas will often change the thriving Sam's Snack Shop into the divine Chez Sam's. And who can forget those chapters in history when a son-in-law's schemes sent the family into Chapter 11.

But, no matter how many blunders the Prince makes, his future is always guaranteed. Even if he squanders the family's fortune, he'll be fortunate enough to get "one more chance". For what daddy could deny his darling Princess the things she wants in life — even if he must pay for them until she's 50.

Once in a *purim,* there are those rare and wonderful cases when the *schlmeil* makes a *mensch* of himself, and father, as well as daughter, are rewarded with a substantial return on their investment. Whoever thought that Millie's Matzoh balls would make a successful mail-order business? (And his mother-in-law, Millie, is forever indebted to him, too.)

But, success or not, daddy can rest assured that his Princess will always be provided for, and the *schlmeil* will know he's not too bad off either, because, as his father always told him (and he should know), it's as easy to marry a rich girl as a poor one.

# BACHELOR PARTIES
## Boys Night Out

A brat and beerfest for the Prince's Last Supper? Rather a meal fit for a king at a favorite local restaurant serving surf and turf preceeded by complimentary chopped liver (which is what the Prince will be by the end of the night if his fiance finds out what's happening).

The Prince's friends have no reservations about going all out for the Prince's final fling. They buy him a portable color TV for his newlywed kitchen. He'll only be watching reruns and eating Lean Cuisine and take-out in that room in the future.

They break in the Prince's new gift by hooking it up to a rented VCR for viewing the last lascivious videos. Next, they ply the Prince with drink and drugs for a few last hours of oblivion. In just a few days his new wife will be oblivious to his pleas to allow him a night out with these characters, which is why the Prince's pals try everything in their power to compromise his character one last time.

No bachelor party would be complete without the presence of the obligatory stripper. Her mission, should the Prince decide to accept it, is to engage the Prince in deviate sexual acts — that is anything other than the missionary position. Often, the Prince's hornier single friends will succumb to the wiles of this wild rented vixen.

They envy the fact that the Prince will now have someone to warm his bed everynight. Of course, a hot water bottle might be cheaper in the long run and probably easier to heat up than Mrs. Jewish Prince.

The party lasts until dawn when the Prince — a "beaten" veteran — joins his buddies for a lox and bagels breakfast — a condemned man's last meal.

# Meeting the Machetenum

The same Prince who strides confidently into the courtroom, and bargains brazenly with his toughest opponents, finds his knees turning to jelly (just like the kind *gefilte fish* is packed in) when a meeting with his future in-laws becomes imminent. His anxiety builds as he worries . . . will her mother wait on him hand and foot like his own mother does? . . . will he stick his foot in his mouth by mentioning how many women he's gone through before settling on their daugher? . . . will her little brother send their plans up in smoke by asking him to get pot for the bachelor party? . . . will his future be questionable if he doesn't have all the right answers at this modern day inquisition? If you're among these panicky Princes (and if you're not, you must be marrying a shikse ) use this handy guide at your meeting with the *machentum.*

| Inappropriate Questions | Appropriate Answers |
|---|---|
| So, what do you do for a living? | I head my own prestigious law firm. |
| How much money do you make? | Enough to take care of you in your old age. |
| What does your father do? | Do? He's a Rothschild. |
| Do you have any brothers or sisters? | Yes, and my brother, the doctor, is interested in meeting your other daughter. |
| Where do you plan to take our daughter on your honeymoon? | Anywhere she likes as long as there are phones so she can call you everyday. |
| Where will you two live after the wedding? | Right here with you. |

**What's a Jewish 10? A 3 with a father who has 7 million dollars.**

# MAKING USE OF THE FAMILY JEWELS — Getting to Yes

> **Q. What is the only thing a Jewish Princess goes down on?**
> **A. The escalator at Neiman Marcus.**

This old joke may be funny — but its absolutely not true. There are many ways for a Prince to entice his Princess into the boudoir. Whether for lust or love, having lots of money and all your own hair helps. But, even without these powerful aphrodisiacs, Princesses can be persuaded. You just have to know which buttons to push.

**NOTE: The authors of this book fought with their consciences (and their husbands) about whether or not to reveal Royal Erogenous Zones. However, they have agreed to expose a few of their trade secrets for the benefit of Princessdom.**

## JAP EROGENOUS ZONES

**The Ear** — For maximum response when nibbling the Princess' ear, make sure her lobes are laden with Karat plus diamond studs. She'll consider you the real stud, if you're lucky.

**The Neck** — A playful nuzzle may have some effect. But if you're removing strands of emeralds and rubies, she'll consider you much more precious.

**The Cleavage** — Covering her with kisses here and there might do the trick. But if you cover her with a silk and satin peignoir, she might consider letting you remove it.

**The Navel** — Sensuous touches of the tummy might turn her on. But give her a coat of lynx bellies and she will consider warming up to you.

**The Inner Thigh** — Passionate pecks in this zone can work wonders but you'll always be wondering if a dozen roses would make her consider being more open with you.

**The Bottom of the Foot** — Caressing her sole can put you in step with the Princess' inner soul. but, after a shopping spree at Maud Frizon, she might consider playing footsie with you.

# COUNTRY HOUSE, CITY HOUSE
## Of Mice & Mortgages

Even before the marriage vows are spoken, the Prince loses all say in matters domestic. His Princess sets about redecorating this bachelor apartment with a vengeance. First to go are the Hadassah baroque *tzatskes* his mother brings back from annual trips to Israel. Afghans crocheted by old girlfriends and Indian throw pillows left over from college days are the next casualties. Peach and grey replace navy and rust and Baccarat and Waterford grace the shelves where once only bongs and stash boxes were found. Thus begins the mandatory three-year stint in the city for the royal newlyweds.

The Prince enjoys walking to the office, meeting friends for dinner and capitalizing on all the culture surrounding him in his urban abode. Obviously, the Prince is content with his upwardly mobile status. Not so the Princess! She has outwardly mobile designs (and we don't mean her hips!). It's not that she's unhappy with city life, it's just that she thinks she would be more happy with suburban living. Since her best friend Helene's move to Scarsdale she's afraid of getting left behind.

So, she convinces the Prince that he's tired of the city, too. Soon he's reading the real estate section instead of the sports pages. The standing of mortgage rates suddenly become more important than the standing of the Mets. After looking long and hard for the perfect palace, they finally find the house they can both agree to call home. He's convinced they can almost afford it, and she's convinced that it's a much nicer place than Helene's.

While the Princess redecorates yet again, the Prince ponders the mysteries of landscaping. In an uncharacteristically economic move, the Prince decides to take care of all the outdoor chores himself. One trip to the local hardware store convinces him otherwise. After all, didn't his ancestors leave the old country so that he would not have to grow up to till the soil? *He* should be reaping the benefits of his move, too. And after all, isn't he much closer now to the golf course?

Since delegating the landscaping, the Prince decides to try his hand at being a back yard chef. After one go-around with the Weber, he's on the phone ordering a self-cleaning gas grill, and his Princess ends up doing the grilling anyway. While bombing at nurturing his garden, the Prince isn't a total failure in suburbia. Nine months after the move, he's nurturing a little Prince of his own.

# For the other side of the story . . . read

# The Jewish American Princess Handbook!

By the same authors, this book, first published in 1982 has become a Jewish humor classic with over 120,000 books in print.

Available in bookstores everywhere or order direct from the publisher.